The Politics of Indust

COLIN CROUCH was born in 1944 and educated at
the London School of Economics and Political
Science and at Nuffield College, Oxford. He is
now a lecturer in sociology at LSE. He is the
author of *The Student Revolt* (1970), *Class Conflict
and the Industrial Relations Crisis* (1977) and of
articles and Fabian Society pamphlets in the
fields of social stratification, industrial relations
and social policy, and editor (with L. N. Lindberg
and others) of *Stress and Contradiction in Modern
Capitalism* (1975), of *British Political Sociology
Yearbook*, Volume III: *Participation in Politics*
(1977) and (with A. Pizzorno) of *The Resurgence
of Class Conflict in Western Europe since 1968*, two
volumes (1978). He is a former chairman of the
Fabian Society.

BERNARD CRICK is Professor of Politics at Birkbeck
College, University of London.

PATRICK SEYD is Lecturer in Politics at the
University of Sheffield.

Political Issues of Modern Britain
Editors: Bernard Crick and Patrick Seyd

Colin Crouch

The Politics of
Industrial Relations

Fontana/Collins

First published in Fontana 1979
Copyright © Colin Crouch 1979

Set in Linotype Times

Made and printed in Great Britain by
William Collins Sons & Co. Ltd, Glasgow

The Politics of Industrial Relations is published in hardback
by Manchester University Press

To my parents

Contents

Editors' Preface

This new series aims to put into the hands of the intelligent general reader concise and authoritative accounts of the major issues of British politics today.

Writing on politics has often suffered from being either strident polemic or ephemeral journalism or else from being academic monographs too technical or theoretical for the general reader. This series hopes to fill an important gap – for it is more difficult to find reliable accounts of what happened ten or twenty years ago than fifty – by covering the issues which opinion polls and experts have judged to be the major issues of contemporary British politics.

We say 'issues' deliberately and not *problems*. Perhaps, indeed, beneath all these explicit issues, election slogans, public worries and press campaigns, there are fundamental and implicit economic and social problems. Theories, whether Marxist or Capitalist, are not lacking to explain them all and to put them all in a 'correct theoretical perspective'. Our aim is more modest and precise: to remedy the lack of books that give accounts of those concerns which might reflect forces more fundamental, but will appear as concrete issues to ordinary people in everyday life. These books will be about politics and not political science.

Each book will cover three main topics: (i) a brief summary of the origins of the issue and fuller account of its history since the Second World War; (ii) an account of its institutional setting and of the pressure groups associated with the issues; and (iii) an account of what should be done and what is likely to happen. We ask each author to be as objective and as balanced as possible on the first two topics, but as polemical and as stimulating as he or she thinks fit on the third.

The series aims to achieve the same high standards of

judgement but also of brevity that have been typical of the Fontana Modern Masters series. It aims to fulfil much the same function: both to be an introduction to the general reader and to be a way in which a specialist in one field can communicate with a specialist in another. If we may draw an analogy, we have briefed our authors to attempt that demanding but non-technical level of writing that is typical of the *Political Quarterly* at its best. Yet while the series is primarily intended for the general reader, students of history, politics, economics and social administration will find that the books fill a gap. They reflect a growing concern in the academic study of politics to look first at actual issues, rather than at institutions or methodologies.

If new editions are warranted, the complete books will, of course, be revised. But each time there is a reprint, we will ask the author to update the section on policy, on what is to be done. Thus each reprint will be topical while the edition places the issue in a deeper historical and institutional setting. We hope that this novel feature of the series will help it to be a contribution to what Walter Bagehot once hoped for from Parliamentary debates, 'the political education of mankind'. For that education seems at the moment so often to suffer from books which are a strange mixture of abstract theory and instant polemic. Issues need studying in an historical context if we are to act sensibly and effectively; and act we must.

Bernard Crick
Patrick Seyd

Author's Preface

Industrial relations provides a crucial arena for observing a more general phenomenon in British politics: the challenge posed to characteristically liberal British institutions by the country's declining economic position. Historically that liberalism has combined security for established elites with an advanced level of rights for subordinate members of the society – a combination which is possible only if some kind of 'headroom' is available to accommodate these potentially conflicting forces. Initially such headroom was provided for Britain by its unique position as the world's first industrial nation and as a major imperial power. In the decades since the Second World War the decline in both these factors has become increasingly rapid, but for several years the country was shielded from the implications by sharing in the unprecedented rise in prosperity experienced throughout the industrial world. Indeed, it was during the post-war period that this distinctive liberalism reached its most advanced development.

Within industrial relations liberalism has taken the form of a very minor level of legal restraint on the activities of organized labour; a system of collective bargaining based on *ad hoc* deals and compromises in which management exchanged concessions at the lower levels of pay increases and working arrangements for undisputed strategic control of industry; and a trade union movement which, while reasonably responsive to its members' demands, was content with its narrow area of uncontested power and raised no major challenges to the political and economic order. As the level of economic growth became increasingly inadequate at providing the room for manoeuvre which these compromises required, they became increasingly dependent on the unreal headroom of inflation. Inflation in turn led to balance-of-payments and foreign-exchange crises, entailing in their turn successive waves of government intervention.

While its particular forms have varied, this intervention of the state has had a consistent purpose: to orchestrate the economy – and indeed the society – more effectively in the pursuit of economic success, and to challenge the apparently expensive compromises in the interests of a new system of order. These attempts have been intermittent, though in very recent years they have become almost continuous, and they have rarely been systematic. However, they have gradually led to important changes in major institutions and have generated major conflicts with the patterns of established interests which they have encountered. In particular they have resulted in a politicization of industrial conflict of a kind which it was a major function of British liberalism to avoid.

This book traces the history of these developments over the varied experiences of the decades since the last war, demonstrating how the present pattern of conflict has been reached. It also considers, in Part Two, the positions now of the main actors in the industrial relations field: employers, Britain's creditors, trade unions, workers of various kinds, governments of both major political parties. What affects the respective powers of these different groups? How have they come to adopt their present stances? What parts have they played in the various institutional innovations which we have witnessed? Consideration of these questions leads to the discussion in Part Three: What are the major alternative courses being offered during this period of rapid change? Which of them are most likely to be followed, and with what consequences?

In an appendix readers will find certain statistical data of interest to the theme of the book: on inflation, unemployment, industrial disputes and trade-union membership. For permission to reprint these I am grateful to the Department of Employment and (for the details of union membership) to the *British Journal of Industrial Relations*. I am most grateful for the assistance of Mrs Joyce

Williams, who typed the bulk of the manuscript and of Tom Richardson, who helped correct the proofs. I am deeply indebted to my wife, Joan, for helping me make many of my thoughts more intelligible; and to Daniel and Benjamin for behaving themselves while I was writing.

Colin Crouch
London School of Economics
and Political Science
September 1978

Abbreviations Used in the Text

ACAS	Advisory, Conciliation and Arbitration Service
APEX	Association of Professional, Executive, Clerical and Computer Staffs
ASSET	Association of Supervisory Staffs, Executives and Technicians (now ASTMS)
ASTMS	Association of Supervisory, Technical and Managerial Staffs
AUEW	Amalgamated Union of Engineering Workers
BEC	British Employers Confederation (now CBI)
CBI	Confederation of British Industry
CPPI	Council on Prices, Productivity and Incomes
DEA	Department of Economic Affairs
DE(P)	Department of Employment (and Productivity)
EEC	European Economic Community
EEF	Engineering Employers' Federation
EET/PU	Electrical, Electronic, Telecommunications/Plumbing Union
ETU/PTU	Electrical Trades Union/Plumbing Trade Union (now EET/PU)
GMWU	General and Municipal Workers Union
IMF	International Monetary Fund
JRC	Joint Representative Committee
LTE	London Transport Executive
NALGO	National and Local Government Officers' Association
NBPI	National Board for Prices and Incomes
NEDC	National Economic Development Council
NIC	National Incomes Commission
NIRC	National Industrial Relations Court
NUM	National Union of Mineworkers

NUS	National Union of Seamen
TGWU	Transport and General Workers Union
TUC	Trades Union Congress
UCS	Upper Clyde Shipbuilders

PART ONE

Origins and Context

Chapter 1

The Post-war Period
(1945 to the late 1950s)

The Second World War provided an important watershed in the development of British industrial relations. This does not mean that suddenly everything changed: important continuities reaching back to the nineteenth century were carried through and helped shape the post-war period, while certain changes had already begun to appear in the 1930s. But several major developments can be dated back to the war: (i) the existence of full employment; (ii) the involvement of trade unions in government policy-making bodies over wide areas of the economy; (iii) acceptance by all major political parties of a policy of trying to keep industrial relations out of political controversy; (iv) a similar acceptance of a commitment to construct a welfare state. Dating from slightly earlier was (v) the emergence of a centralized trade-union leadership which was prepared to reach understandings with governments and which then had the power to enforce acceptance of the results on its membership.

(i) The full-employment criterion was of major importance to the unions and to labour generally. Few things weaken the strength of organized labour more than a high level of unemployment; workers fear taking steps of which their employers will disapprove if they can be easily dismissed and replaced by someone else, and they stand little chance of making successful demands for higher wages if there are unemployed men outside the factory gate prepared to take work at almost any price. Before the Second World War industrial society had been characterized by alternating periods of boom and slumps, in which years of high employment were followed by those in which economic activity declined and many were thrown out of work. In particular the 1920s and early 1930s had seen a prolonged slump throughout the industrial world; unemployment in Britain had reached 20 per cent of the labour force and trade-union organization had been massively weakened.

The war brought full employment because of the enormous needs for manpower of the war effort, for both the armed forces and arms production. But after the war the official commitment to maintaining near-full employment was retained as a result of government acceptance of the economic policies advocated by Lord Keynes, an acceptance motivated at least in part by fear of massive social discontent if there were any return to the conditions of the 1920s. It is beyond the scope of this book to discuss these policies in detail, but in essence the government committed itself to keeping economic activity at a level which would maintain full employment by increasing spending on defence, social services and other public services during periods of recession.[1] (At the same time, it was supposed to reduce its spending if the economy became over-heated, threatening inflation.)

The war-time coalition government accepted this commitment for the post-war period, and this was pursued by both the Labour and Conservative administrations that followed. This was therefore a development of enormous importance to the unions, improving their chances of being able to organize workers and make demands to improve conditions of employment. Not surprisingly, several employer interests were uneasy, one of their most important sources of power over workers having been weakened. Some voices predicted that wages would get out of control and that there would be no discipline over labour. In fact, developments of this kind did not begin to cause significant problems for capital for several years; some, though not all, of the reasons are to be found in other items in the war-time changes.

(ii) The involvement of union leaders in government bodies was an ambiguous development.[2] Certainly the Trades Union Congress and the leading unions had sought it, and they had made some progress in the pre-war decades. With the war the number of bodies on which the unions were represented expanded considerably, and this pattern held in the post-war period. At the same time, the mass of social legislation passed in those years led to the establishment of a range of tribunals, supervisory committees and so forth at regional and local levels to oversee the new services, on many of which trade unionists were represented. This enabled the unions to exercise influence within many areas from which they had previously been excluded; it gave them access to information about how the political and economic system worked; and it brough: a new stature and acceptance to their position in society.

On the other hand, this involvement fell short of any bodies which exercised real control over the economy, or was limited to the token representation of trade unionists on organizations whose fundamental mode of operation remained entirely unaffected. (A major example of this, occurring under the post-war Labour government, was the inclusion of trade-union leaders among the directors of the Bank of England after its nationalization. Neither taking the Bank into public ownership nor putting union leaders on its Board did much to affect the place of the Bank as spokesman for the interests of the City of London.) A further problem with union participation was that over many of the areas concerned the unions had no particularly distinctive policies, at least none that had emerged from the life and work of trade unionists at all levels. Although often the unions began to develop policies in response to the fact of participation, the seriousness and distinctiveness of the union role frequently remained unclear.

A major motive of the government in extending participation was to reduce the area of conflict between the unions and capital by taking union leaders into a structure in which they could be persuaded to co-operate and adopt the views of government and industry on economic priorities. During the war these priorities were clear enough and agreement relatively easy to achieve. (During the First World War far less had been done to integrate labour in the war effort, and there had been massive industrial conflict during the war itself. This had been followed by the bitter years of the 1920s and 1930s, and a continuation of intensive conflict with the reappearance of war was deeply feared.)

Labour's new status was symbolized by the appointment of Ernest Bevin as Minister of Labour in the coalition government.[8] Bevin was General Secretary of the Transport and General Workers Union, was the leading figure in British labour and had played an important part in the General Strike of 1926. As Minister he acquired vast powers over the allocation of labour to the war effort. These powers invaded traditional rights of control over work and reduced individual workers' rights to change jobs at will. It is doubtful whether organized labour would have acquiesced in this had not such a figure as Bevin been the responsible Minister. Direction of labour also meant suspending the usual market processes of wage determination, which in turn affected the ability of trade unions to bargain over pay levels. There were therefore legal restrictions on bargaining, including making strikes illegal, offset by new institutions for arbitration to resolve conflicts peaceably. In practice the laws against strikes were singularly ineffective; the number of unofficial strikes during the war was very high indeed, and few attempts were made to use legal powers against them.

The detailed controls over bargaining and strikes did not long survive the war; but – in conditions where, with the ending of hostilities, consensus between labour and capital on priorities became less easy to secure – the attempt at incorporating union leaders in government machinery did survive. An attempt at assessing the importance of these mechanisms in the 1950s will be one of the tasks of this chapter.

(iii) Acceptance by the political parties that industrial relations should be taken out of political controversy was similar in intent to the incorporation of union leaders discussed above: emphasis would be placed on areas of consensus and agreement in order to contain conflict and, in particular, to prevent disputes – which would inevitably arise in relations between employers and workers – from spilling over into the political arena itself, increasing the intensity of social divisions. The policy was not without its paradoxes. A party 'truce' on industrial relations could remove the subject from political *controversy*, but the increased involvement of the unions in government machinery hardly removed it from politics. The implications of this tension eventually became felt, though not for two decades.

Removal of industrial relations from political conflict suited the interests of most of those involved. Relations between the unions and the Conservative Party had been particularly soured during the Depression, especially during and after the General Strike. It had been the unaccommodating policy of a Conservative government towards the coal miners which had precipitated the strike; the government had pursued a particularly belligerent line during the strike; and after the unions' defeat it had pressed its victory home in the Trade Disputes and Trade Unions Act 1927, which had hampered the unions' work in various ways.[4] In 1940 Winston Churchill, a leading member of the 1926 government, now Prime Minister of a nation at war, badly needed the support and co-operation of the same trade-union leaders whom he had humiliated fourteen years previously, and his government was happy to see the whole area removed from the political agenda. As we shall see, he followed the same strategy as a peacetime Prime Minister in 1951.

The Labour Party and the unions were also content with such a policy. (On industrial relations issues at this time the party had few interests separate from those of the unions.) While it has been stressed above that unions had been weak during periods of high unemployment, they had also experienced periods of economic upturn when they could deploy bargaining strength; and the skilled trades, which accounted for a large proportion of organized labour, were less affected by overall unemployment levels than the less well organized unskilled workers. There were therefore times and situations when unions could achieve something for their members through bargaining within the existing industrial system. They had a strong interest in maintaining the autonomy of this area of collective bargaining and were deeply suspicious of any invasion of it by government. Governments had been predominantly representative of interests hostile to organized labour, and the unions did not trust them. Even less did they trust the judges whose job it was to administer any laws which parliament passed. Time and again over the preceding century the courts had interpreted the law in ways hostile to union interests; repeatedly the unions had subsequently put pressure on governments to change the law to remove the effect of the judicial decision, and their frequent success in this had then often been undermined by further legal decisions.

The reason for this strange pattern of developments can be readily explained.[5] The Common Law of England had undergone major development during the early years of the industrial revolution, in response to the interests of *laissez faire* capitalism. This form of capitalism operated through the free exchange of goods and services in a market with which nobody 'interfered'; that is, government did not intervene in the detailed process of trade, and no social interests organized themselves in order to try to change the terms of the contract that would emerge from the free market bargain. As will be explained more fully in Part Two, workers are automatically at a disadvantage in such a process, and their main attempt to offset this has been to form organizations – trade unions. But the formation of organizations breached the rules of free contract and was illegal. The strategy of British unions in the face of this problem was to put pressure on governments to change the law so that their activities were no longer illegal, and at certain points governments responded positively to this pressure.

Why did they do so, when these unions had such little real strength? It may be significant that the English political system had a long history of dominant elites coming to terms with emerging antagonistic groups, compromising with them on the condition that they accepted the main outlines of the system. This policy was extended to labour. It was made possible by the dominant position of Britain in the world. Its industrialization had started much earlier and proceeded further than that of other powers, and its vast empire ensured captive markets for Britain's industrial goods and a secure supply of cheap food imports. Concessions to organized labour could be afforded because of an absence of tight international competition – and they were also likely to spare the country the upheavals experienced by various continental countries which tried to exclude labour from political influence. Most significantly, the most important measure which admitted the unions to legality – the Trade Union Act 1871 – was passed, by a Liberal government, not long after the Act which began to extend the suffrage to certain manual workers.

Concessions of this kind were made, by no means always without struggle, somewhat before areas of strength had been established which might become troublesome; they were not made where they were unnecessary. Thus, while governments were prepared to recognize rights to organization where workers had already fought for them, there were no attempts at offering official assistance to organize to groups experiencing difficulties in doing so (the majority of workers remained outside unions for most of the nineteenth century).

It is important to note the form taken by the concessions of 1871, for they provided the mould for labour legislation over the following century, in fact for exactly 100 years.

The unions were not given an elaborated code of positive rights, but specific exemptions from the legal penalties which they would otherwise automatically incur at Common Law. This had two main consequences: it left the Common Law tradition itself intact – the cause of the continuing conflict between the unions and the courts; and, more important, it established the primarily liberal system of industrial law. Union rights derived from the strength they could develop and assert themselves, rooted in the actions of their members rather than (as in the North American and several continental systems) being defined by government and dependent on government's will. The unions were therefore invited into the liberal political system of nineteenth-century Britain, able to enjoy rights where they could autonomously lay an effective claim to them and trying to avoid detailed intervention by the law. The unions thus developed as defenders of a system of this kind, and were happy to accept a national truce on political involvement in industrial relations.

(iv) The final war-time development of importance was the consensus on the welfare state. This provided a further admission of working-class interests into politics, though in a manner that did not challenge radically the established power structure. It therefore gave added reality to the consensus to which all interests would seem to be committed in the newly emerging pattern of institutions.

(v) To all these developments of the war period is to be added the increased centralization of the trade-union movement which had occurred in the previous decade. In contrast to the other labour movements of industrial Europe, British unions had grown from the base upwards. Groups of workers, particularly in the skilled trades, had developed a power of local organization and had progressed from there to construct national organizations, the weak co-ordinating body of the TUC and, finally, the Labour Party. National-level bodies had been more important in organizing semi-skilled and unskilled workers, because their labour-market strength was that much weaker, but the decentralized model was the basis of the movement as a whole. The typical pattern elsewhere in Europe was for labour to organize itself first as political parties – communist and socialist – and these in turn created union movements. In Britain it was entirely the other way round.

The relative importance of national union leadership and local (works or district based) groups varied with the economic situation: when unemployment rose, the strength of local groups was eroded, and it was left to the national organizations that they had generated to fight defensive battles. During the great Depression of the 1920s this process had become more than usually prolonged. The shop-floor groups which had risen to prominence in several sectors during and after the First World War lost their power base; the national organizations remained to try to maintain the framework of national agreements in order to prevent competitive wage cutting by employers. As the economy recovered in the late 1930s, it was at this national level that the unions were able to start meaningful bargaining again; the shop-floor movement had not recovered its organization. This same national level of leadership had its position further strengthened by participation in government machinery during the war. The domination of the movement by a centralized national leadership was thus a relatively unusual feature of British unionism of the war years.

The pattern of industrial relations bequeathed by the extraordinary arrangements of war-time mobilization therefore contained a typical British patchwork of measures combining to form a new compromise between the classes. Labour's strength within polity and economy was considerably strengthened by full employment and, more ambiguously, by union participation in official machinery. The potentially disruptive implications of the former were held in check by the generation of a new national consensus (based on war priorities, the construction of the welfare state, the incorporation of the unions, the ending of party-political conflict over industrial relations) which included union leaders who were, in turn, powerful enough to impose order on their members. But this consensus and this incorporation were not organized and imposed by vigorous state intervention, but emerged informally through the relatively relaxed and liberal institutions characteristic of British politics.

The Labour government

The election of a Labour government immediately after the war intensified further two mutually counter-balancing aspects of the above pattern: the power of the unions and their incorporation. The unions held a dominant position in the policy-making of the Labour Party, and they gained from this influence: legislation was passed abolishing most of the provisions of the Trade Disputes and Trades Unions Act 1927, and the number of bodies on which unions had representation increased as the administration was committed to establishing new institutions of government economic planning. At the same time the incorporation of union leaders was increased because their commitment to the success of the party in office strengthened their acceptance of government-determined priorities.

At first, events developed as might have been expected, with unions, industry and government collaborating in the rather obvious priorities of post-war reconstruction. However, as early as 1948 the first signs of instability appeared.[6] Largely because of rapid re-armament following the government's participation in the Korean War, the economy was over-heating, leading to a rising level of inflation. Reluctant generally to deflate the recovering economy, the government sought to persuade the unions not to take advantage of the tight labour markets that were developing. The leaders responded favourably and were able to impose restraint on their members. It should be noted that they accepted restraint with reluctance; an initial statement of the need for wage restraint by the Prime Minister, Clement Attlee, angered the unions, and the eventual agreement was reached cautiously and with less restraint than Ministers had hoped for. The election of a Labour government had not reduced the unions' preference for autonomy in the area of collective bargaining where they had established their main strength – especially as the government commitment to full employment had considerably increased the unions' bargaining strength.

But the factor that undermined the agreement on restraint was not the reluctance of the union leaders; under conditions of full employment the shop-floor base of several unions had recovered its strength. The policy was tolerated for two years, but by 1950 the delegate conferences of several unions had rejected any renewal of the agreement. The government's need to move to a more or less formal policy of wage restraint had in the first place suggested that the balance of the post-war consensus would not always ensure economic stability; the shop-floor revolt showed that an element of that consensus itself was unreliable – the domination over their unions of the main leaders.

The Conservatives

The size of Labour's victory in 1945 had led many people in the Labour movement to believe that its domination would now be virtually permanent, and the Conservative victory in 1951 came as a surprise. The Conservatives were still mistrusted following the experience of the inter-war years (the war-time coalition was seen as an exception), and it was widely believed that they would not honour the full-employment commitment. Nevertheless, on the new government's election the TUC General Council passed its famous resolution offering support and co-operation. For their part the Conservatives also moved to ramify the class consensus. Sir Walter Monckton, who was not a professional party politician, was appointed Minister of Labour. He interpreted his office as being to mediate between employers and unions during industrial disputes, and to add conviction to this role he distanced (as far as possible) his political position from that of the Conservative cabinet of which he was a member. An important priority of the government was to prevent the growth of widespread industrial conflict of the kind that had threatened social stability in the 1920s, and in particular to prevent the escalation of industrial conflict into politics; politics, and especially Conservative politics, therefore had to be seen to be studiously avoiding intervention in industrial relations.

It might seem a strange expedient for a department of state to be partly removed from the government of which it was a part, but it was not entirely without precedent where the Ministry of Labour was concerned.[7] The Ministry, which had originated in 1893 as the Labour Department of the Board of Trade, had been established as a force for encouraging industrial peace through conciliation, mediation and arbitration. Its character had been developed by an important group of civil servants and various outsiders who served voluntarily as mediators, rather than by the politicians of any particular government. The Ministry had adapted itself to, and in turn helped to shape, the essentially voluntarist nature of British industrial relations. Although a department of government it did not work primarily through law but by cajoling, persuading, leaning on the parties to a conflict, in theory helping them to reach the solution which they would have found by themselves had not the conflict escalated. The Ministry thus contributed to that tradition of avoidance of legalism and the insulation of industrial disputes from politics which suited the interests of different groups at different times, but which was preferred by virtually all those involved at the time of the war-time and post-war consensus.

During the Depression the Ministry's role had in fact been rather diverted from its typical pattern of stabilizing and encouraging established procedures and established organizations of both capital and labour. It connived at the erosion of national agreements – a policy which suited the employers at a time when the maintenance of agreed national minima was the only strategy available to the unions for resisting wage cuts. However, with the economic recovery of the late 1930s the Ministry had reverted to its former role, and during the war it was, under Bevin's leadership, a major force in the construction of national-level bargaining. Under the Labour government, Bevin's main successors were former trade-union officials (George Isaacs and Alfred Robens).

These were able to retain the confidence of the unions, and when the Conservatives returned to power Churchill was anxious to retain the progress that had been made in integrating union leadership with government and industry – hence the appointment of someone like Monckton, who was able to keep union confidence while the rest of the government was embarking on policies disapproved by the unions.

The Conservatives were greatly assisted by favourable developments in the economic cycle. After the temporary crisis of re-armament for the Korean War, Britain was able to share in the massive growth in world trade which ensued as countries recovered from the ravages of war and began to rebuild their economies, under the aegis of a new economic stability guaranteed by dollar leadership of the exchange rates and by Keynesian demand management. The desperate pressures of the war had encouraged in all industrial countries a massive burst of technological innovation, initially at the service of the armed forces. When hostilities ended, the enormous potentialities for peace-time application of these innovations could be developed, and this provided the basis for a period of great economic progress, gains in productivity and rises in living standards.

This period lasted broadly from the early 1950s to the late 1960s, becoming designated 'the age of affluence' or 'the affluent society'. It wrought changes in many areas of life in societies whose immediate past had seen two world wars and the great Depression, and not least in industrial relations. An almost continuously expanding national product enabled nearly everybody's living standards to rise year by year. In a static or declining economy no one group can advance except at the expense of someone else; if the size of the national product is constantly expanding, everyone can have more without anyone else losing. There are still potential conflicts of distribution: such a system does not necessarily do anything to reduce inequality, and if wealthier groups gain the lion's share of the new resources the degree of inequality will actually increase. But these problems tend to be concealed behind the universal advance.

There was an additional element in the prosperity of the 1950s. The government was known to be committed to maintaining, through the full-employment policy, a high level of demand. This gave employers confidence that they could expect economic growth to continue without major interruptions by the periodic slumps of the pre-Keynesian economy. They could therefore concede wage claims with little fear of being priced out of markets.

In retrospect the 1950s appear as a decade of decline and wasted opportunities for the British economy. The world leadership which it had retained until the 1870s had been slowly disintegrating as other nations industrialized, taking advantage of Britain's experience and improving on it; this process accelerated with the decline in the country's position which had occurred during the Depression and the Second World War. The United States emerged as the obvious leader of the Western world, militarily and economically, displacing Britain. (However, Britain retained many of the trappings of its previous position – in particular a high level of spending on armaments and the role of sterling as a reserve currency – which probably served to weaken its position further among the countries of Western Europe.) Further, while slumps in the old sense were avoided, governments failed to pursue policies which avoided alternate bursts of expansion and deflation, the situation which became stigmatized as 'stop-go'. In general, Britain's growth rate was considerably slower than those of most of its competitors outside the USA, and its productivity improvements were unimpressive. (Some of the reciprocal influences between these factors and the structure of industrial relations will be discussed in Part Two.) But these unfavourable consequences did not become salient until the 1960s, and did not produce major problems for a further decade. At the time the rates of growth, the degree of economic stability and the advance of prosperity were measured against the experience of the past; and superiority over the rest of Europe was virtually taken for granted. Affluence and stability therefore added a new element to the supports of the post-war consensus that was not really foreseen at the time of its forging. The potentially inflationary consequences of full employment combined with free trade unions could be held at bay if growth absorbed the main impact of union demands. In fact, there was a significant shift in the basis of the integration of the industrial relations system as the 1950s progressed. Seen from the perspective of 1945 the main safeguards of order in the post-war world would be institutional and consensual: a national system of bargaining under a centralized trade-union leadership which broadly accepted the priorities of government and industry as a result of the needs of post-war recovery, the urgency of post-war reconstruction and their links with the new party of government. Gradually all these items were reduced in significance. As we have seen, even by 1950 the sovereignty of the national union leadership had been put in doubt; in the years to come, further significant changes were to occur on this dimension, and the unity of the union leadership itself was to be disrupted. The integration of union leaders with government and industry was further reduced as the immediate priorities of the post-war years receded, as the Conservatives dismantled much of the apparatus of economic planning, and by virtue of the Tories being in office rather than Labour. As these elements declined, so prosperity rose in significance as a major basis of cohesion. The shift was gradual, always relative, but eventually of considerable importance in its implications.

However, while it is appropriate to place the main emphasis on growing prosperity in an account of the stability of industrial relations in the 1950s, it would be misleading to ignore the occasional signs of tension which gave some indication of what lay ahead. The delicate balance between full employment, price stability and economic growth was by no means maintained with perfect success. In addition, a British government had to pay attention to a further economic variable: the need for a stable exchange rate for the pound sterling, made a particularly tricky task by the continuing role of the pound as a world reserve currency.

The government placed high priority on the maintenance of full employment as an important guarantor of social stability; it was therefore prepared to tolerate some rise in the level of inflation in order to protect this goal. However, if inflation or a deterioration in the balance of payments led to a deterioration in confidence in the currency, necessitating expensive support by the Bank of England to maintain the exchange rate, the government would introduce deflationary measures, raising unemployment slightly and checking growth (the stop-go phenomenon). But wages were not always highly sensitive to minor adjustments in the employment level, largely because of the very institutional arrangements of collective bargaining which formed part of the consensus. Bigger increases in unemployment would threaten stability; but so would attempts by the government to interfere in collective bargaining given the universal commitment to keeping politics out of industrial relations (and *vice versa*).

A problem of this kind confronted the Conservative government as early as 1952, and it tried to have recourse to a third weapon: use of its own administrative powers to regulate economic variables without direct recourse to the level of employment. But, given the low level of development of economic planning, few such devices were available. All that lay readily to hand were the powers of the Minister of Labour to refer back the decisions of wages councils. These councils, consisting of representatives of employers and workers and certain 'independents', have the task of fixing minimum pay levels in industries with particular problems of low pay. Their decisions have to be ratified by the Minister, who cannot amend them but must merely accept or reject – in the latter case asking the council to think again. In 1952 Monckton referred back decisions affecting councils in twelve industries. The councils refused to amend their recommendations and the Minister had to accept them – since it was out of the question that the workers involved should receive no pay increase. His initial action outraged the unions, both because it involved 'picking on' groups of particularly low-paid workers, and because the Minister was, albeit timorously, interfering with the autonomy of established institutions. The wages councils, by refusing to amend their awards, also stood by the tradition of voluntarism.

It was a minor incident, causing temporary ruffles on the calm waters of the politics of British industrial relations, but it illustrated the strength of the commitment to voluntarism by the unions and others involved in the institutions, and also demonstrated the paucity of weapons in the government's armoury. Given the fine balance of the economic variables involved, the problem was certain to recur.

The government's next search for a solution involved trying to strengthen the consensual mechanisms of the post-war system: it sought a voluntary agreement with employers and unions on wage and price restraint. In 1955 it approached private employers and the nationalized industries to secure agreement on price restraint, as a prelude to the more difficult task (for a Conservative administration) of approaching the TUC. A Budget favourable to industry was introduced to help secure agreement. But the same Budget angered the TUC, who replied that restraint was possible only if policies of social justice were pursued, and that in the meantime the unions would follow a strategy of unfettered collective bargaining. This has remained an element in the response which the unions make to overtures from governments of whose policies they disapprove. Clearly, the consensus was already showing signs of erosion; the government was Conservative, and the unions, having risked unpopularity with their members in 1948-50, were anxious to avoid doing so again, especially as the strength of shop-floor organization was growing in several industries.

By the following year the government had turned to a quite different tack. In May the Chancellor of the Exchequer, Harold Macmillan, attacked trade unions as being largely responsible for Britain's inflation, and later that year the government published its White Paper *The Economic Implications of Full Employment*,[8] which at last questioned the commitment to full employment if price stability was to be pursued. But the document proposed few specific measures; the government feared any major breach with the unions which might lead to conflicts of the kind familiar in the inter-war years. Instead, apart from promising to pursue pay restraint in the public sector, it threw the burden on to employers, urging them to resist excessive wage claims.

The engineering and shipbuilding employers accepted this challenge and resisted major national wage claims.[9] There were lengthy strikes. At first the government followed its declared policy and, breaking with one of the tacit principles of the consensus, allowed national strikes to proceed without a flurry of conciliation activity by the Ministry of Labour. After some weeks, however, the traditional reluctance to risk the escalation of conflict supervened; the government offered conciliation and the employers were pressed to accept the appointment of courts of inquiry. The latter operated on the usual lines of seeking a compromise – no other guidelines were available to them – and the result was a large increase in wages. But the courts of inquiry, while following the tradition of arbitration, expressed concern in their reports that there had been no means whereby they could have taken account of the 'national interest', and proposed the establishment of an impartial body which would be able to pronounce on this and to which negotiators could have reference. While any attempt at defining a national interest would be an inherently political task, this was watered down by the insistence that the body would be independent of government and that negotiators and arbitrators would be under no obligation to take note of it. In other words, what was being proposed was not so much a change towards state intervention as an attempt at developing a more formal and explicit consensus.

The government responded by appointing a Council on Prices, Productivity and Incomes, comprising three members who became popularly known as the 'three wise men'. They had the task of keeping the general development of the economy under review and issuing periodic reports. The TUC gave the Council a cool but not hostile welcome, commenting that until the government pursued different social and economic policies unions could do nothing other than pursue free collective bargaining.

Sterner actions were, however, imminent. A major sterling crisis in September 1957 led the government to take highly orthodox restrictive measures. Protection of the rate of exchange had priority over the pursuit of growth, the maintenance of full employment and preserving good industrial relations. An increase in unemployment was expected to reduce inflationary wage settlements in the private sector, while the government committed itself to resisting demands in the public sector. When the CPPI subsequently endorsed this action, the TUC broke off relations with it and ceased to co-operate with it for the rest of its life.

These moves clearly, if temporarily, ruptured part of the post-war consensus – the maintenance of full employment. But it was the policy of resistance in the public sector which attracted the most overt political conflict, for it involved the government in over-ruling various settlements achieved through established negotiating machinery. Matters came to a head in 1958 when disputes loomed in two important areas: the London buses and the railways. Both were sectors in which strikes would have an immediate effect on the public, and it was usually assumed that a government would be blamed for a strike that caused general inconvenience. In the event the government chose to confront the busmen but to compromise with the railway workers.[10]

There was wisdom in the choice. The busmen's union, the Transport and General Workers Union, was claiming a higher differential for central London over outer London crews – a claim which was unlikely to attract the strong loyalty of *all* the union's London bus members. The dispute between London Transport and the union went first to arbitration, which found against the union. The TGWU rejected this result because it suspected that government pressure had been put on the arbitrators, and it called a strike. The government was doubly protected from odium; the dispute was ostensibly between the LTE and the union, and in any case the arbitrators had found against the men's claim. In effect, the union was asking the government to allow London Transport to overturn the arbitration decision. The strike was prolonged. The Labour Party opposition identified itself heavily with the union. The TGWU called on the TUC to give active support, on the grounds that it was fighting the battle of all unions against government interference in collective bargaining.

This was refused; many union leaders still remembered the General Strike of 1926, which had seen a heavy defeat for the unions, and they feared any strike 'against the government'.

Eventually the strike collapsed. The government had not only secured a 'victory' on wage restraint; there was considerable evidence that public opinion supported the government and blamed the union for the disruption, to the surprise of many Ministers. The Conservatives took note that for them, though perhaps not for the Labour Party, there might be more votes to be gained than lost from industrial disruption. Indeed, the different positions of the Conservative and Labour Parties on the bus strike were seen as contributing to the former's sweeping victory in the general election of September 1959. One limb of the post-war consensus – the priority on industrial peace – had become potentially unstable.

However, the government did not immediately make any major shift in policy. When it faced the railway dispute shortly afterwards, it returned to the politics of compromise, despite its general stance of public-sector resistance.

Chapter 2

Years of Growing Tension
(the late 1950s to 1968)

By the late 1950s a heterogeneous set of developments in British industrial relations converged to threaten the viability of the post-war consensus. The government's difficulties in balancing the almost inevitably conflicting *desiderata* of economic policy have already been discussed. A second major factor was the gradual rise in the number of industrial disputes throughout the 1950s. This rise continued in most industries throughout the 1960s as well, but after 1957 it was offset by a factor which for a while deflected political attention away from this question: from that year the number of strikes in coal-mining began a lengthy decline, partly because the industry was in decline and partly because of a change in the wage payment system which had the effect of reducing the number of small disputes. Mining had typically been responsible for the majority of strikes, and this decline was enough to mask the completely opposite trend taking place in other industries.[1]

A particularly significant aspect of the rise in the number of disputes was the growing proportion of unofficial strikes among them. This capacity of workers to take action by themselves reduced the importance of the national union leaders who were party to the (albeit shrinking) consensus with government and employers. No separate record of unofficial strikes was kept until 1961 – the decision to do so then was itself a reflection of increased concern about the question. It is therefore not possible to say at what rate unofficial strikes increased during the 1950s, but by 1960 they had reached 98 per cent of total stoppages – remaining at roughly that proportion until declining slightly from the late 1960s.

Not only did this development reduce the importance

of the national leadership; in those unions which were highly responsive to their members the positions of the leaderships themselves reflected the new militancy. This partly explains the strong position taken by the ship-building and engineering unions and the TGWU in the 1956-8 period. The shift in the centre of gravity of British unions towards the shop floor was not an unprecedented development; as was stressed in the previous chapter, this had historically been the case. It was, however, new in terms of the pattern that had developed since the late 1930s – though even then it has to be remembered that the level of unofficial strikes during the war had been extremely high, rendered insignificant only by war-time controls that reduced their effectiveness.

A third factor was a by-product of the ballot-rigging case affecting the Electrical Trades Union.[2] In 1957 a group of union officials alleged that the communist leadership of that union was maintaining its position only by mis-reporting and misrecording the results of branch elections. There followed a long and bitter struggle culminating in victory in the law courts for those making the allegations and the expulsion of the ETU from the TUC in 1961 until it had put its house in order. The issue did considerable damage to the public reputation of the unions in general, and in the eyes of some observers it highlighted a general failing in the legal liability of union officers for their con-duct of affairs.

These developments, together with the political out-come of the 1958 bus strike, led sections of Conservative opinion to revise their attitude to the post-war consensus. The first visible sign of this was the publication in 1958 of *A Giant's Strength* by the Inns of Court Conservative and Unionist Society. This claimed that the unions had become 'over-mighty subjects' and proposed various measures for subjecting them to legal regulation, includ-ing: restriction of the right to strike to officially registered unions; an automatic public inquiry and cooling-off period before any strike could be legal; making workers' protective practices actions liable at law; and provision for strike ballots to be called, but only by union members wishing to *end* a strike.

Significantly, Ministers offered no support to the document, and in 1959 and 1960 the Conservative government did nothing to take advantage of its new electoral strength to press measures hostile to the unions. There were only two events of significance. In a national newspaper dispute in 1959 there was evidence that the government had deliberately withheld the Ministry of Labour's conciliation service for fear that this might result in too high a settlement. Second, the Industrial Disputes Order, a legacy of war-time controls, was annulled and replaced by a much weaker measure. The Order had made it possible for terms achieved in one set of negotiations to be extended to other areas, and in principle it could be enforced against workers as much as employers. In practice it was not possible to impose such a device on the hundreds or thousands of workers who would be involved in a dispute, and it was only the unions who ever made use of the provision. As a result, the employers successfully lobbied government for the annulment of the measure.

Both issues – the printing dispute and the Industrial Disputes Order – produced controversy between the government on the one hand and the unions and the Labour opposition on the other. The conflicts were minor, but they did relate to a common theme, and one that had featured in the earlier disagreements. The elaborate network of arbitration and similar institutions had originally been established with the aim of containing and limiting outbreaks of conflict. However, under the post-war conditions of near-full employment these same mechanisms could be used by unions to secure wage concessions in excess of what industry felt able to concede. The government therefore embarked on some limited dismantling of the institutions as part of its counter-inflation strategy.

The pay policy, 1961-4

Government policy in the late 1950s thus hovered around a range of different measures for tampering with or alternatively reinforcing the post-war consensus, none of which was pursued with any consistency. By 1961 certain new developments brought sharper pressures to bear. The continuing decline in the British economy against its competitors was finally becoming evident, and blame was widely attributed to stop-go policies. Several groups associated with industry began to show an interest in economic planning as it seemed to be practised in France. At the same time, other voices were advocating the adoption of a more or less formal incomes policy. At home, the Council on Prices, Productivity and Incomes advocated in its final report some kind of incomes tribunal – making a sharp break from the free market policies which it had followed in earlier reports. Abroad, the Organization for European Economic Co-operation produced a report on the problem of rising prices which included Britain in a list of countries in which incomes policies would be a valuable weapon in combating inflation.[3] The two developments were linked: it is difficult to envisage a form of economic planning which did not include an attempt at planning incomes, and the unions would have been unlikely to accept incomes policy unless it was in the context of a general planning exercise in which they were involved.

Any intellectual developments tending in this direction were sharply strengthened by the sterling crisis of July 1961, which was again attributed to excess wage pressure. This time, in addition to general restrictive measures the government declared a six-month freeze on pay rises – to be enforced by government decision in the public sector but left to employers to apply in the private sector. To follow this, the government proposed the establishment of a National Incomes Commission, to which contentious pay agreements would be referred for public comment. At the same time initiatives were taken to launch a national planning body, the National Economic Development Council. None of the measures had very sharp teeth, beyond the government's commitment to enforce incomes restraint on its own employees. The NIC would only examine a pay settlement after it had been concluded, and it had no powers to enforce its decisions. Similarly the NEDC would have no powers to direct economic policy, but would act as a sounding board and an opportunity to integrate union leaders with the thinking of employers and the government.[4]

Organized employers co-operated with these initiatives – though individual firms often preferred to reach agreement with the unions over a claim and avoid a strike rather than adhere rigidly to some national norm, since there were no sanctions on them to do otherwise. The unions' position was more difficult. It was their members' pay, and not employers' prices, which would alone be affected by the controls in the first instance. Free collective bargaining, the touchstone of union activity, was clearly being threatened. On the other hand the unions, and especially the TUC, had long adopted a policy of accepting and indeed urging participation in government decision-making bodies; it was a way of ensuring that the union view was not ignored, and it was participation of this kind which contributed much to the influence and standing of trade-union officials. Against this, the NIC was not at this point being equipped with actual powers.

In the event, the unions had little difficulty in deciding to reject any involvement with the NIC, but by a majority within the TUC they agreed to participate in the NEDC – the minority arguing that the government was only involving the unions in planning in order eventually to implicate them in incomes policy, a view for which there is considerable support.

The government's strategy at this time can be usefully

assessed in the light of a point made in the previous chapter (p. 23): in seeking to involve unions in a national consensus by integrating them in tripartite machinery, the government was putting in jeopardy the insulation of industrial conflict from politics (itself an element of the consensus), and this difficult tightrope could only be walked if the areas of involvement were outside the arena of political conflict. The NIC and NEDC both constituted further ventures across this tightrope. The former fell because by invading the unions' treasured preserve of free collective bargaining it was too controversial; indeed it was only by limiting its powers to virtually nothing that the government was able to introduce it without a major politicization of industrial relations. The NEDC, however, walked the tightrope successfully, being of all the institutional innovations in this area of policy since 1957 the only one which, two decades later, has survived three changes of government. In the words of one observer, writing of the early 1970s: '. . . even when relations between TUC and ministers were most strained, NEDC still served as a meeting point – if sometimes as a battleground – between the two sides. The fact that it survived the storms of this period proved its strength if not its effectiveness.'[5]

Very early in its life, however, in 1963, the NEDC did become involved in difficulties with the unions when, in its publication *Conditions Favourable to Faster Growth*, it referred to the importance of many incomes of all kinds rising 'substantially less rapidly than in the past'. Several left-wing union leaderships objected strongly to the acquiescence in the phrase by the TUC representatives on the Council. Since then, governments, employers and unions have been careful to use the NEDC as a forum for discussing medium and long-term problems, not immediate emergencies. Employers and governments have continued to use it to persuade unions of the problems of the economy, but whether this has had an effect on union bargaining behaviour it is difficult to judge; to make such an assessment would require an entire research project – one not easy to carry out. As for the NIC, it staggered on, making a total of four reports – all after the event (though in the case of one, on the vast engineering industry, it brought out an interim report while negotiations were still in progress), and in all but one case (on university teachers) being boycotted by the unions concerned. Its reports raised issues of importance and carried significant implications for the requirements of an incomes policy that would be effective; but the Commission's direct impact on industrial relations was very small, and none of its activities created as much political interest as its original establishment.[6]

Of greater immediate importance was the government's determination to abide by its posited norm of 2½ per cent wage increases in the public sector. Here the government could do more than exhort. In the case of its direct employees it could simply decide not to pay large increases – provided it was prepared to face strikes and a deterioration in industrial relations. Where public corporations were concerned, it could refuse to advance additional resources to finance wage settlements which it regarded as excessive – subject to the same provisos. If a public corporation decided to pay an increase and absorb the cost (or raise its prices) there was little the government could do but cajole or apply private pressure to board members. It had to resort to the former in 1961 following a settlement outside the norm in the electricity supply industry. The Prime Minister, Harold Macmillan, formally criticized the settlement in the House of Commons, though taking care at the same time to disavow any step towards a statutory incomes policy (on the grounds that this would constitute fascism). The TUC complained that this intervention constituted state interference in collective bargaining, but in practice the government was taking no action at all.

In certain cases affecting its own employees, however, it did take steps to keep them within the norm. In adopting this policy towards the public sector the government was acting on the theory that competitive pressure would restrain pay in the private sector, while it must through its own administrative action ensure restraint in the non-competitive public sector. As many private industries, including in 1963 the engineering industry, made settlements which paid no regard to the norm, this theory wore rather thin; a more likely consequence of the government's action was the artificial restraint of public-sector pay, a tactic it had used before and which resulted in distorted wage and salary differentials between public- and private-sector jobs. A more pressing source of the government's policy was the fact that the public sector, or more narrowly still, government employment, was the only area where it possessed powers which it could use – reflecting the government's inability and unwillingness to adopt a comprehensive incomes policy. It could also claim that within government service it was acting simply as an employer of labour, and not as the state, and that therefore its interventions did not constitute political interference in industrial relations. However, the more the government used the public services as an arena for implementing the policy of the norm, the less convincing such arguments became. These matters came to a head in a prolonged dispute with the postal workers, a few months before the 1964 general election. The case provided a great contrast with that of the London busmen in 1958. The claim in question was a simple wage demand by a publicly popular group of low-paid workers. They had never struck before; they were being restrained by government at a time when many other groups were securing larger increases despite the norm; and the government was clearly the men's antagonist in the case. The dispute dragged on and ended in a complex compromise, but it was quite clear that public sympathy lay with the postmen.

While the closing years of Conservative government were, in the industrial relations field, mainly marked by disputes over incomes policy, a small but significant development also took place in the area of law reform proposals, just as had been the case in 1958. And, again as in

1958, the matter was triggered by a legal case, *Rookes v Barnard*.[7]

Mr Rookes, an employee of British Overseas Airways Corporation, had been dismissed from his job because of his refusal to join the Draughtsmen's and Allied Technicians' Association, and he took the union officer concerned to court. It was generally assumed that the immunities of unions from Common Law liability in the course of an industrial dispute covered cases of this kind. However, following the historical pattern described in Chapter 1, the courts redefined the scope of the immunity to render the officers concerned liable. Again following the historical pattern, the TUC called for government action to restore by statute the position which had been believed to exist before the court's decision. More generally, the court's action was seen as reflecting a shift in 'public opinion' which felt that the unions were becoming too powerful. The lobby within the Conservative Party which had supported the policies in *A Giant's Strength* became active again. By calling for action on *Rookes v Barnard*, the unions had created an opportunity for those demanding that trade-union law as a whole should be placed on the political agenda – with the implication that this should lead to a diminution of unions' rights. The government responded ambivalently, as it had done so often before when presented at once with a chance of reducing the power of the unions and a risk of provoking exacerbated politicized conflict. The Minister of Labour, John Hare, proposed a Royal Commission to look at *all* aspects of industrial relations law, including the unions' complaint with respect to *Rookes v Barnard*, but, curiously, the Commission would not be appointed until after the forthcoming general election. Interestingly, while the government did not survive the election, the promise of a Commission, with some slight modification, did.

How are the politics of industrial relations under the Conservative governments from 1951 to 1964 to be assessed? In Chapter 1 a certain shift in the basis of the consensus was described – from reliance on the institutional incorporation of the unions to dependence on mass prosperity, with a few minor breakdowns of the consensus along the way. This chapter has described a further shift – though again its relative nature must be stressed; neither incorporation nor affluence were removed from the scene. The shift occurred because the underlying weaknesses of the economy were making it less easy for an effortless progress in prosperity to absorb all conflict. Indeed, significant voices were beginning to argue that the avoidance of conflict was impeding the progress of prosperity: workers' restrictive practices, which reduced productivity, were passing unchallenged, and wage demands were being too readily conceded, in both cases in order to minimize conflict.

In part, the resultant shift can be seen as an attempt to refurbish the institutional integration of the unions, to shift the balance back to the pattern prevailing before affluence had started to play its part: the NEDC and the attempts at an agreed incomes policy were all part of such a pattern. But this was no return to the 1940s; the conditions of the war period were no longer present. There were no agreed priorities of reconstruction, no Labour government, no centralized union leadership in near-total command of its membership. The attempt was therefore more reliant on formal mechanisms and overt government action. But this in turn threatened the delicate balance referred to in the previous chapter: the post-war settlement managed to achieve an increased involvement of industrial relations with political institutions without political controversy, the tacit consensus being sufficiently strong. Precisely the opposite was the case in the early 1960s.

The Labour government, 1964

The chances of securing consensus seemed to improve considerably in October 1964 when the Labour Party returned to government after thirteen years in opposition. The commitment to planning sat more comfortably on Labour's shoulders; and, more important, the party had its strong links with the unions. While these links are frequently commented on, it is useful to ask in what they actually consist, and also why the Conservatives' links with business do not seem to provide the same advantages.

The Labour Party's relations with the unions do not merely, or even primarily, refer to the fact that Labour leaders and union leaders are often on good personal terms as a result of this involvement in the same movement, though the personal commitment to Labour policies by dominant individuals within the union movement has certainly been significant at several important junctures. More relevant has been the dependence of the Labour Party on the unions; a dependence on their votes in support of the party's leadership at annual conference, on their financial contributions and on their manpower support for the party at local level. This dependence of party on unions leads the unions to be more prepared to accept actions by a Labour government which they would resent from the Conservatives. This is so for two reasons. First, because of its dependence on them a Labour administration is on balance more likely to introduce measures favourable to the unions and less likely to introduce unfavourable measures than are the Conservatives, so the unions have a stronger interest in helping a Labour government to stay in office. Second, should a Labour administration begin to intervene in industrial relations, the unions feel they have a better chance of restraining it and limiting its actions.

As to why the Conservatives' links with organized business seem to matter less, it is necessary here to anticipate a point that will be made at greater length in Part Two: most of the pressure in this area of policy is on the unions to restrain wage demands and to alter certain working practices. In the long run employers stand to gain from this since, if successful, such a policy reduces wage costs and makes control over labour easier. True, individual companies may often prefer to make settlements with their unions and maintain good relations with them and their work-force, rather than have government policy make life difficult. But the interests of industry *as a whole* will be served by successful wage-restraint policies. Similarly, the price controls and measures favourable to the unions, which may have to be offered as a *quid pro quo* for restraint, are an exchange which is necessary if government and industry alike are to secure their central goal of wage restraint.

For unions the situation is very different, since incomes and restrictive industrial relations policies strike at the heart of their main activity; their co-operation is therefore more difficult to seek. Of course, industry may reach the point where it feels more inconvenienced than helped by a particular policy, and may virtually withdraw support, especially if the opposition is offering a more attractive alternative; but for most of the time their support for policies of restraint, at least at the level of national organizations, is fairly easily gained. The same may not be true for policy areas outside industrial relations.

Certainly the Labour government in 1964 started off with considerable goodwill. While industry would have preferred to deal with the Conservatives, it seemed impressed with the new government's commitment to planning, which was then newly in favour. British industry and commerce were in fact in the process of forming a new centralized organization, the Confederation of British Industry, which would make relations between government and business easier to operate, especially in the new period of planning.

Relations with the unions were not without their difficulties. Labour had opposed the Conservative incomes policy on the grounds that it had concerned incomes alone and not prices, and that only a government committed to 'social justice' had a right to introduce wage control. Labour claimed that it would pass muster on both these points, but that was of relatively little interest to unions whose main concern was to keep government out of free collective bargaining. Labour could not rely automatically on the support of the union leaders as it had done in the 1950s, when the majority of unions could be guaranteed to back the party's leadership against left-wing critics at the annual party conference. The change which had taken place in the unions, discussed in the last chapter, had also made itself felt at the level of political relations. This had been shown most notably during the debates which had rent the party in the wake of its election defeat in 1959. The left had tried to commit a future Labour government to unilateral nuclear disarmament, while the right (under the leadership of the party leader, Hugh Gaitskell) had attempted to remove from its constitution the party's commitment to public ownership of the means of production, distribution and exchange. For the first time since the war the leadership had been opposed by a significant group of trade unions, led by Frank Cousins, General Secretary of the TGWU.

The unions could not therefore be taken for granted, and for some time before the 1964 election it seemed possible that Labour would be deprived of its prize of being able to claim the ability to secure an agreed incomes policy. However, the unions' desire to assist Labour in an election victory was strong. Further, they wanted an end to the recurrent threat of higher unemployment implied by the 'stop-go' economy, and therefore supported the increased planning which Labour claimed it would introduce – and which implied at least some co-ordination of wage bargaining with wider economic policy. It was in fact under the slogan 'the planned growth of incomes' that Cousins threw the support of the TGWU behind Labour's proposed version of incomes policy. And in 1964 Cousins cemented the links further by becoming Minister of Technology in the Labour cabinet.

The new government's first step in industrial relations, under the leadership of the Secretary of State for Economic

Affairs, George Brown, was to secure a tripartite 'declaration of intent' under which government, industry and unions committed themselves to the pursuit of planned economic growth, and income and price restraint. At the same time a National Plan for the economy was being prepared. It then set up the machinery for the incomes policy: a National Board for Prices and Incomes with members drawn from industry, unions and 'independents' under the chairmanship of Mr Aubrey Jones, an industrialist and former Conservative Minister. Unlike the NIC, the Board would investigate pay increases and price increases before they were implemented, and it was equipped with a large staff to enable it to make reports on a wide range of issues, not just the occasional ones as had been the case with NIC. A further difference was, of course, the inclusion of prices as matters for separate reference. But the NBPI shared characteristics with the NIC in that it would examine claims and rises against the criterion of a government-established norm; and, in that it had no powers to enforce any of its decisions – it would operate by exhortation alone.[8]

From early on it became clear that the completely voluntary nature of the policy would be inadequate for the government's purposes. The weaknesses of the economy were becoming an increasing problem; a heavy balance-of-payments deficit had developed in the Conservatives' last years, and (perhaps exacerbated by mistrust of a Labour government) the holders of sterling exhibited continuing lack of confidence in the currency. One response to these pressures would have involved the devaluation of sterling and probably a policy of controls over imports and capital movements accompanied by more *dirigiste* planning to try to construct a stronger economy through state action. This would have meant a more radical break with previous economic policy than the government was willing to risk. Another alternative would have been a severe bout of deflation, taking the heat from the economy and probably restoring confidence but at the expense of the government's commitment to sustained growth and the avoidance of unemployment. While there were some concessions to this option, the government mainly tried to restore confidence by strengthening the incomes policy, using the threat of deflation as the alternative as an inducement to the unions to comply with stricter restraint. During the sterling crisis of summer 1965 it asked the TUC both to agree to a minor element of statutory control over pay agreements and to set up a vetting machinery of its own to keep member unions in order.[9]

The former involved a legal obligation on unions and employers to notify the Department of Economic Affairs of pay claims and proposed price increases, so that the government could decide whether or not to refer the matter to the NBPI. In the event of a referral, implementation of the increase could be delayed by up to three months – after which it could be paid even if the Board reported adversely. Even this modest increase in regulation was viewed with disfavour by the TUC as a further step towards state control of collective bargaining; but the unions were sufficiently moved by fear of impending financial crisis to acquiesce both in the planned legislation and in the idea of TUC vetting machinery. The government undertook not to implement the new law if the voluntary machinery was effective.

These measures only bought time. In summer 1966 there was an official strike by the National Union of Seamen in pursuit of a wage claim which the government saw as in excess of the incomes policy. The strike caused an immediate crisis in its obvious impact on Britain's trade, and this was accompanied by a political crisis as the Prime Minister, Harold Wilson, charged that the strike had been fomented by communist agitators – an unprecedented case of Ministerial intervention in a dispute. The strike was eventually resolved by a settlement which went outside the government's policy guidelines, thus further weakening the incomes policy. The combination of trade crisis, deteriorating industrial relations and obvious weaknesses in incomes policy led to a further massive sterling crisis. This time the government responded with both heavy deflation and a radical strengthening of incomes policy. The former ruined the government's planning strategy, since it would no longer be possible to meet the growth target; stop-go had returned, if indeed it had ever been surmounted. The latter involved measures not unlike those of 1961: a pay freeze for six months followed by a longer period of severe restraint. There was, however, one major difference in that the new policy was statutorily enforced. A Labour government was now involved in the business of preventing (or, rather, postponing) pay increases by law – a development quite contrary to the understandings of the post-war consensus – while the deflationary measures meant the death of the National Plan, an important element in the attempted construction of a new consensus.

Sections of the union movement and the Labour Party had dissented from the incomes policy from the start, and particularly after the introduction of a statutory element in 1965. This opposition advocated the remaining alternative policy: devaluation, import controls and increased state planning. After the 1966 crisis it won new adherents. Frank Cousins resigned from the government and the TGWU dissociated itself from the incomes policy. However, a majority within the TUC still stood by the government and took no action to disrupt the new policy. It suspended the operation of its own vetting machinery for the duration of the freeze, but this was less a protest and more a reflection of the fact that the machinery was irrelevant if no pay rises could be granted; the incomes policy committee was re-established when the freeze was lifted.

Inevitably statutory controls of the kind now introduced involved the use of specific orders to prohibit the implementation of pay awards reached in breach of the law – several unions, notably the Association of Supervisory Staffs, Executives and Technicians (ASSET), refusing to recognize the freeze or period of restraint. These orders, often against small groups of not highly paid workers, created considerable acrimony between the government and sections of the Labour movement. Some basic elements of the old policy of keeping politics out of industrial relations were being broken.

The year of freeze and severe restraint was followed by a further period of only slightly relaxed controls, though again the General Council of the TUC was prepared to co-operate. However, developments not unlike those of 1950 had taken place; the unions' membership was becoming increasingly restless at restraint. Further, the gains to be achieved through having a Labour government were diminishing as most of its original policies were abandoned. At the 1967 Trades Union Congress the policy of compliance with government policy was rejected. This did not mean total confrontation. Most unions continued to try to find loopholes in incomes policy as a means of securing larger increases rather than take on the government in a legal battle – there were enough loopholes to make this profitable, and few unions relished the prospect of open conflict with government. Highly characteristic of British unionism was the TUC's own response to the changed situation. It continued to monitor pay claims according to a norm; but this was now a norm selected by the TUC itself, consistent with its own expansionary economic policy rather than the government's own norm. Eventually the incomes policy committee (by 1970 renamed the collective bargaining committee) changed the emphasis of its work from regulating claims to advising unions on bargaining policy and trying to co-ordinate bargaining in terms of agreed priorities – a prominent issue being an attempt at securing exceptional increases for the low paid.

The statutory policy also became unpopular with employers; it included limitations on price increases, and it impeded their freedom to make pay awards which suited their needs. They continued to co-operate with the policy, seeking (successfully) some added flexibility in rewarding highly paid employees, and sought what scope they could for making productivity agreements. But they came to place increasing emphasis on an alternative strategy: the reform of industrial relations legislation, which will be discussed in the following chapter.

An assessment of incomes policy[10]

Since the policy became unpopular with the government's own party, the unions and the employers, what compensating gains did it bring? Estimates of the overall effect of an incomes policy are extremely difficult to make: one can never be certain what would have happened if the policy did not exist, nor that any changes occurring during the period of the policy actually resulted from its operation. The period of total freeze and severe restraint was highly, if temporarily, effective. At other times the government's official norm was usually exceeded by the overall level of pay rises, but it might still be possible that that level would have been greater in the absence of the policy. From time to time the NBPI made estimates of its relative success in this respect.[11] Other writers have been less sanguine;[12] it is generally accepted that the policy 'dammed up' claims during its period of operation, but, to continue the metaphor, that the ending of controls breached the dam, resulting in a flood of claims. This is because statutory (or voluntary) restraint cannot obliterate the fundamental market (and bargaining) forces leading to pressure for higher pay. Similar arguments apply to price rises.

Arguments of this kind have more to do with the future of a pay policy than its present, and they do not weigh particularly heavily with governments facing an immediate crisis to which pay restraint seems the least troublesome solution. They are inclined to believe that there will probably be ways, when the time comes, for engineering a gradual phasing out of the policy rather than an abrupt end. The Labour government did plan such a transition, since in 1969 it relaxed but did not end controls and planned certain changes in the structure of the policy which would make it more acceptable to the unions, though there was also a notable pay 'explosion' at the same time. Whether or not this can be attributed entirely to the lifting of incomes policy will be examined more closely in the following chapter.

The incomes policy did not only aim at simple pay and price restriction. The NBPI was a sophisticated investigatory instrument that backed its decisions on particular cases with detailed examinations of practices in individual companies. It could therefore comment on ways in which prices could be restrained and pay increased through measures for improving efficiency as well as through simple control. These and other policy goals became possible by means of the exceptions to the norm which the policy provided. There were grounds on which workers could be awarded pay rises in excess of the established limit, and these included:

  (i) cases where specific improvements in productivity had been achieved;
 (ii) attempts at improving the income of the low paid;
(iii) cases where employers experienced difficulty in recruiting labour; and
 (iv) groups of workers whose pay had fallen significantly out of line with comparable groups.

Later, at the urging of the Board, the government added:
  (v) the need to restructure pay within a firm – largely a euphemism for increasing the incomes of managerial staffs.

Of these criteria the Board was reluctant to use (iii) and (iv) since they seemed to provide loopholes for all the usual practices of pay determination that were considered to be associated with inflation. Trying to overcome specific labour shortages by making pay increases at a time of general labour scarcity was considered by the Board to be inevitably inflationary except in very special cases; while granting rises on the basis of comparability re-erected one of the principal devices of traditional collective bargaining. The low-pay criterion also gave the Board difficulty. Politically this was a highly important criterion, since Ministers would often claim that helping the low paid was an aim which incomes policy could fulfil but which collective bargaining could not tackle. In practice the Board found it difficult to define low pay and experienced some conflict between this criterion and its own policy of strengthening pay differentials where it felt they corresponded to a rational structure of skill and responsibility. Towards the end of its life, however, when the government was trying to restore the popularity of incomes policy, it made some specific references on low-pay issues to the Board. The presence of the criterion did help give the issue of low pay publicity and political relevance. It certainly seemed to affect the unions; partly to meet the challenge that collective bargaining could not help the low paid, and partly to take advantage of the scope for exceptional increases that the criterion provided, several unions made low pay an important bargaining goal during the late 1960s, both in terms of a national aspiration expressed through the TUC, and in specific negotiations.

The remaining criterion for exceptions – productivity improvements – was initially treated cautiously by the Board as it was uncertain how to assess them and feared they could be used as a guise for straightforward pay increases. However, as time passed the Board grew more confident, came to see positive benefits in the scope which productivity agreements offered for increasing the efficiency of British industry, and perhaps on occasions used productivity as a device for finding a compromise in awkward situations. A productivity agreement was defined by the Board as:

one in which workers agree to make a change, or a number of changes, in working practices that will lead in itself – leaving out any compensatory pay increases – to more economic working: and in return the employer

agrees to a higher level of pay or other benefit.[18]
The device was used to secure reductions in manning levels; to induce craftsmen to relinquish some of their job controls and protective practices; and to introduce new methods of working, often requiring more effort by workers. The concept of the productivity agreement had originated in the Esso Oil refinery at Fawley, where a highly ambitious scheme had been studied and written up by Allan Flanders, an academic industrial relations specialist.[14] D. A. C. Dewdney, managing director of Esso, was a member and sometime joint deputy chairman of the NBPI.

In his account of the Esso experiment, Flanders had stressed two important factors. First, the device enabled management to take the initiative in bargaining, proposing changes in job organization to the work-force rather than passively receiving pay claims. Second, there was an attempt at involving the workers in a joint pursuit of efficiency – on management's terms – rather than bargaining with them at arm's length in the customary way. The NBPI tried to encourage these features in the productivity agreements which it fostered. Since productivity agreements provided the most likely means of securing a pay increase in excess of the norm, both employers and unions took advantage of the opportunity offered and the number of agreements rose considerably during the period of pay policy, despite the misgivings of several unions at the prospect of relinquishing precious job controls. Even unions which officially did not accept the incomes policy continued to make use of this criterion. For example, in 1968 the TGWU (which was no longer co-operating with the government) found that an agreement, which it had reached with the municipal bus companies, was being blocked following adverse findings by the NBPI; instead of waging a national confrontation the union began to make productivity deals with individual bus companies. As the unions learned to take advantage of the productivity criterion, so the nature of the bargains changed from ambitious management-led attempts at involving workers to more straightforward bargaining, exchanging work changes for pay.

The widespread adoption of productivity bargaining was probably the most significant achievement of the incomes policy, though it was largely temporary. By the early 1970s, with the NBPI gone, with employers beginning to believe that they had conceded more in pay than they had secured in work changes, and with the unions more reluctant to accept manning reductions as unemployment rose, the practice became unpopular. Productivity bargaining has, however, survived as an occasional feature of bargaining, sometimes recognized in subsequent incomes policies.

The above discussion has probably suggested that national-level debates over industrial relations issues shifted from the formal political arena to the Board. This is only partly true. Throughout the period a major issue was shaping over the role of law in industrial relations. There was also political controversy each year as the government introduced the latest stage of its increasingly unpopular policy. Finally, while the NBPI carried out investigations and made recommendations, the government retained the initiative at two crucial points: the Board could launch an inquiry only if the case was referred to it by Ministers, and Ministers reserved to themselves the decision whether and how to act on the recommendations of the Board. The whole process was highly political. At times Ministers would make dramatic token gestures to impress public opinion or overseas creditors – as, for example, when Barbara Castle, Secretary of State for Employment and Productivity, made a major effort to restrain the prices of bread and beer, or when she actually secured a temporary wage *reduction* of one penny an hour for building workers following a report by the NBPI that a pay agreement reached in the industry had not been justifiable under the criteria of the policy. On other occasions, negotiations which would have led to potentially damaging disputes were permitted to produce agreements which were not referred to the Board, despite doubts as to their acceptability. These factors all contributed to the politicization of conflict over incomes.

Developments after 1968

The year 1968 constitutes a watershed in the development of the conflict over industrial relations and incomes policy in several respects.[15] In the previous November the pound sterling had finally been devalued during yet another foreign exchange crisis, and in circumstances which rendered it an additional policy to heavy deflation rather than an alternative. The government had sacrificed nearly all its original policies – planned, sustained growth; a voluntary incomes policy; even, to a certain extent, full employment – to defence of the dollar parity of sterling. Now even this had gone. Opposition to the government's policy within the unions, the Labour Party at large and the Parliamentary Labour Party, was spreading. Although the government's majority in parliament was secure, the abstention of a growing group of back-benchers from votes on the incomes policy was a considerable embarrassment. The government's national popularity was also sinking for various reasons, reflected in colossal losses in by-elections and local elections.

Furthermore, little remained of the post-war balance of policies and forces which had sustained consensus in industrial relations. The special links which Labour claimed to enjoy with the unions had been used so heavily to badger the unions into accepting wage restraint that a few union leaders began to ask openly whether the relationship was worthwhile. The idea of a tacit consensus on economic priorities had become very attenuated, while from about 1967 the government took fewer steps than its Conservative predecessor to try to establish more formal arrangements; the NEDC played only a minor role. That the policy of keeping industrial relations out of politics had collapsed has been made abundantly clear in the above narrative account, but this is perhaps seen most clearly in the fate of the Ministry of Labour, the institution which embodied the ideal of non-political conciliation. At first, the voluntary nature of the incomes policy, and the fact that it was in any case supervised by the Department of Economic Affairs, enabled the Ministry to maintain its traditional role, though this was punctured at intervals by aggressive speeches, usually condemning unofficial strikes, by the Minister, Ray Gunter (himself a former union leader). In 1968, however, responsibility for the increasingly statutory incomes policy was transferred to the Ministry, and the tensions between its role as non-partisan conciliator and as the department responsible for a policy which expressed a distinct view on pay issues became acute. Many unions felt they could no longer trust mediation or arbitration organized through its auspices. The change in name of the Ministry – to the Department of Employment and Productivity – at the same time symbolized the transition: the department was now much more closely identified with the pursuit of over-all government strategy in industrial relations, incomes and manpower planning.

These changes should not be exaggerated; the number of cases of pay negotiations which led to strikes or became entangled with the NBPI were only a minority, while the conciliation work of the Ministry of Labour was in many cases able to continue, surviving the change to the DEP. And despite the breakdown of consensus, most union actions can be regarded as restrained if examined in terms of what *could* have occurred. There were no attempts at general strikes or similar measures to enforce withdrawal of the statutory incomes policy; no union tried to force an employer to breach a court order made under the Prices and Incomes Acts; as already noted, unions worked through the incomes policy even if they no longer formally supported it. After all, the main demand of the unions was to return to the conditions of free collective bargaining which had existed before; they were therefore anxious not to make the breach with the past absolute. These points are worth remembering when these events are compared with those of the years 1969-75.

But union behaviour was obviously affected by the context in which it now existed. On the one side unions were being pressed by government to act politically by diverting their industrial behaviour to suit the needs of the government's economic policy. This led them automatically to develop their own counter-strategies for economic growth (symbolized in the TUC's Economic Policy Reviews which gradually adopted policies sharply different from those of the government). Unions could no longer bury themselves in industrial activity and ignore overall political economy. At the same time they were coming under increasing pressure from the opposite direction: from rank-and-file members impatient with restraint and seeking higher incomes. The number of strikes, which had been declining slightly, increased sharply from 1968, and well over 90 per cent of them were unofficial. Some unions, in which the leadership was insulated from membership pressure and whose main officers were loyal to the government, resisted this upsurge of resentment; but in many other cases the unions responded by adopting a more militant stand themselves. This was particularly striking in the two largest unions, the TGWU and the Amalgamated Engineering Union. Both elected as their leading officers men who had themselves emerged through the shop-steward movement and who believed in responding to membership demands – Jack Jones and Hugh Scanlon.

The growing significance of unofficial strikes occurred at a fateful moment. In 1968 the Royal Commission on Trade Unions and Employers Associations reported. This had been established by the Labour government following promises made by the Conservatives in 1964. In evidence before the Commission, the representatives of employers' associations had called for new legal controls over strikes, especially unofficial ones. The Conservatives had, since leaving office, adopted such a policy; and the Labour government, anxious to be free of the travails of incomes policy, looked forward to the Commission's report for an opportunity to move in a similar direction, if less radically.

If the period of incomes policy had wrought major havoc with much of the post-war consensus, the policies to which both major parties turned as more viable alternatives in fact did further damage to what remained. This is the final respect in which the year 1968 constituted a turning point in the politics of industrial relations.

Chapter 3

The Collapse of the Post-war System (1969 to 1974)

It has been mentioned in earlier chapters that, from the later 1950s, elements within the Conservative Party began to agitate for reforms in trade-union law which would impose certain constraints on what unions could do. These changes were often presented as removing from unions some of their immunities at Common Law which, it was argued, were not justified under modern conditions, whatever had been the case in earlier decades. In fact the proposals usually went considerably further than this and imposed on unions a positive duty to control their members. Of course, any such move to introduce law into industrial relations would have broken the implicit terms of the post-war consensus, and, in recognition of that fact, Conservative Party leaders set their face against all such policies. But as problems of inflation grew and as the terms of the consensus became more fragile, they began to reassess that view. Released from office in 1964, the party was able to review its policies more radically.

The Conservative conversion to planning in 1961 had never extended to all sections of the party, and in opposition the forces opposing it became dominant. With this the attachment to incomes policy, which smacked too much of government intervention in the economy, was also ejected. The withdrawal from incomes policy was gradual, because the party had been rather firmly wedded to it in government, but it was facilitated by the growing unpopularity of Labour's policy. By 1967 the Tories had made a considerable *volte-face* on their stance of the early 1960s and appeared as a strongly private-enterprise party opposing state involvement in all economic processes, including incomes. This did not mean a reversion to the post-war consensus, though that too had rested on assumptions about the absence of state involvement in incomes. The new Conservative position meant a withdrawal from full employment so that the market would govern income determination, reducing inflation. To accompany this, a Conservative government would stand firm against pay claims in the public sector, and would abandon the idea of seeking conciliation and the avoidance of disputes as the prime goal of industrial relations policy. While the avoidance of inflation was the main aim here, the Conservatives were not unaffected by a realization that strikers were becoming increasingly unpopular, and that government, particularly a Conservative one, might not attract public odium in the event of prolonged conflict.

But the party did not believe that these steps would be enough to secure order in industrial relations. They now officially adopted the policy which a minority of them had advocated for several years: legal measures to make unions more vulnerable at law, to make strikes more difficult and to oblige unions to control their own members. The same ideas were attracting support within industry, though with mixed feelings. Industrialists were attracted by the idea of legal sanctions which would strengthen their control of their work-force, but they feared the damage that would be done to industrial relations if employers became involved in legal actions against their own workers. They preferred arrangements whereby the onus of legal action would be borne by the state. Since one of the motives of the Conservatives in adopting the new strategy was to avoid the detailed involvement of the state in industrial conflict, this alternative was not entirely attractive. However, these differences were submerged in an overall agreement that industrial relations law reform represented the best available alternative to an increasingly disliked incomes policy. The two largest employers' associations within the Confederation of British Industry – the Engineering Employers' Federation and the National

Federation of Building Trades Employers – were, among others, converted to the new policy, and this quickly led to the CBI itself taking the same position.

As mentioned in the previous chapter, in 1965 the Labour government had appointed a Royal Commission on Trade Unions and Employers Associations, under the chairmanship of Lord Donovan. This now received strong representations from employer interests, the Conservatives and others that radical changes were needed in the law, along the lines indicated. Against this, the unions and those favourable to their interests elaborated a sustained defence of the post-war consensus : of the contribution to industrial peace which had been achieved by the tradition of voluntarism; of the dangers of government and the law becoming implicated in industrial relations; of the achievements of free collective bargaining.

It is interesting to note that labour appears here as the conservative interest, as the defender of a *status quo* warning of the dangers of exacerbated conflict. Official Conservatives had originally supported the post-war consensus as in their own interests, reducing the threat to the existing order posed by a militant, discontented labour movement capable of using its industrial strength for political purposes. Now, however, it seemed that these interests had more to lose from the slow, steady erosion of industrial authority that had been occurring than they might under a more sharply conflictual system on legal terms renegotiated in capital's favour.

For its part, the Labour government had publicly accepted trade-union opposition to any new legal measures. In private, however, Ministers were coming to share the view that the rise of shop-floor power was undermining the capacity of union leaders to control their membership, and governments always prefer to deal with simple, unified, centralized organizations. Also, the tendency for major disputes that threatened economic activity to produce sterling crises led Ministers to favour any measures that would make strikes more difficult. The seamen's strike of 1966 had been an instructive experience in this regard. New legal measures might make incomes policy both easier to operate and less necessary: the power of organized labour would be weakened by legal controls; while overseas creditors, who would panic at any simple lifting of incomes policy, might be assuaged if this were accompanied by industrial relations legislation. The government was therefore secretly hoping that the Donovan Commission would propose measures which, while falling short of what the Conservatives were advocating, might usefully be adopted by a Labour administration.

But Donovan did not oblige. Opinion within the Commission was deeply divided, but an important part was played in the shaping of its report by a group centred round members of the 'Oxford school' of industrial relations research, a group of academics who tended to support voluntarism and free collective bargaining: Hugh Clegg was a member of the Commission, W. E. J. McCarthy was its research officer and Allan Flanders submitted a lengthy piece of evidence which figured prominently in the Commission's report.[1] A good deal of the research sponsored by the Commission was also carried out by Oxford academics.

It was largely under the influence of this group that the Commission's report was drafted.[2] This strongly supported the voluntary system – though proposing reforms within its terms – and rejected any major legislative initiative to restrict union activities. It did, however, advocate certain measures for increasing union rights and thereby removing various contentious issues from the arena of conflict. This surprising victory for voluntarism was not achieved without cost: one minor proposal (for removing immunity from prosecution from unofficial groupings of workers who induced others to break their contract of employment in furtherance of an industrial dispute) received the support of a bare majority; other similar proposals attracted substantial minorities; and several members submitted notes of dissent or reservations calling for more radical measures, all broadly along the lines of the Conservative CBI policies though differing in technical detail.

The unions were relieved at the report; industry was dismayed but looked forward to a likely Conservative government which would introduce something more radical; and Labour was denied its best excuse for introducing legislation opposed by its union allies. While various parties, but especially the TUC, launched a programme of post-Donovan voluntarist reforms, the Secretary of State for Employment (Barbara Castle), strongly backed by the Prime Minister (Harold Wilson), began to prepare legislation despite the Commission's emphasis. In the White Paper *In Place of Strife*,[3] published early in 1969, the government announced its intention of introducing a Bill which would institute, alongside several innovations favourable to workers and unions: conciliation pauses and strike ballots (that is, compulsory suspensions of a strike while a ballot was held to test the strength of support for it); investigation by a new Commission on Industrial Relations of inter-union disputes; and the establishment of a compulsory register of trade unions which would make certain minor requirements of union rule-books. Ministers believed that they could persuade the unions to acquiesce in the measure, taking advantage of the party-union links and the concessions to union demands offered as a *quid pro quo*. They had been encouraged in this view by George Woodcock, the retiring General Secretary of the TUC, who had been a member of the Donovan Commission. But the TUC, under the leadership of Vic Feather, the new General Secretary, refused to countenance any legislation of this kind.

The issue was first broached with the unions at the beginning of 1969,[4] and by April there had been no progress. The government, which had decided it could no longer continue with a tough incomes policy, needed some new restrictions on the power of labour in order to placate overseas holders of sterling. In the Budget speech of that month the Chancellor of the Exchequer announced that, pending the main Bill on which negotiations were proceeding, there would be a short Bill comprising just two main items: the measures to deal with inter-union disputes and the conciliation pause for use during unconstitutional stoppages. The announcement of an industrial relations measure in a Budget speech was itself extraordinary, and strengthens the view that it was intended primarily for overseas creditors.

Far from accepting this interim measure more readily, the TUC made it clear that they would not tolerate it. The Prime Minister suggested that the government would not need to implement the Bill immediately if the TUC undertook to amend its own disciplinary powers to enable it to punish member unions which (i) became involved in inter-union disputes and (ii) did not themselves discipline unofficial strikers. The former was acceptable to the TUC, but the latter was not, automatically implying as it did that the workers were always 'at fault'. The TUC offered instead to use its offices to intervene in disputes to try to bring about peace, without prejudice to any judgements on the merits of the case.

Meanwhile, opposition to the Bill was stirring in the Parliamentary Labour Party.[5] An important part was played in this by the large group of Labour MPs who are sponsored by unions. In the past, this group had rarely been known to act cohesively: for example, they were not involved in the various rebellions against the Prices and Incomes Bills. The Industrial Relations Bill proved to be an exception. An increasingly large minority of Labour MPs signified that they would refuse to support the Bill, while the Conservative opposition would oppose it on the grounds that it did not go far enough. The government was faced with a pincer movement: its union 'allies' were opposing the Bill through the channels of government/ interest-group negotiation, while many of its own MPs were opposing it in parliament. Harold Wilson announced his determination to see the Bill through, whatever happened. But shortly afterwards, with the unions holding firm, the Chief Whip, Robert Mellish, informed the cabinet that he could not guarantee a parliamentary majority for the Bill. In a complete reversal of policy, Harold Wilson and Barbara Castle accepted the TUC's 'solemn and binding' undertaking to intervene in disputes on the terms which it had earlier offered. It was a humiliation for the government; the CBI made insulting remarks about the value of the new agreement; while the unions and the Conservatives were, in their different ways, delighted.

The episode is often presented as a major instance of union power over a government, and in many ways it obviously was. At the same time, it should be noted that a crucial part was played by the conventional constitutional power of the government's back-benchers who opposed the measure. While the bulk of these came from the Trade Union Group of Labour Members, it is remarkable that the unions themselves took no steps to provoke this opposition. Although unions often use their MP members to raise more-or-less technical questions affecting their various industries and areas of employment, they have never worked through the Trade Union Group on matters of general policy – partly a reflection of the unions' desire to avoid suspicion of tampering with constitutional processes, but mainly evidence of their preference for affecting policy through their direct access to Ministers, an important element of the post-war consensus.

After the *débâcle* of the Bill, the government spent its final year in office mending its relationship with the unions, strained during the previous years. A new Industrial Relations Bill was introduced in 1970 which would have given the unions many of the new rights proposed by Donovan, with no punitive *quid pro quo*; but the Bill had not passed through parliament before the government fell. Incomes policy retained an element of sanctions, but was flexibly applied, and the whole policy was re-oriented to place the emphasis on breaking down the 'monopoly power' of employers, covering both prices and incomes issues through that channel. A merger was envisaged between the NBPI and the Monopolies Commission.

With incomes policy relaxed, the wage claims that had been 'dammed up' were now brought forward, and the rate of pay rises reached unprecedented levels. These were the years of the 'pay explosion'. The rise in the number of strikes, which had started in 1968, continued, a notable element being the spread of militancy to new groups, especially white-collar workers and low-paid public-sector employees. Particularly prominent among the latter was a prolonged strike by municipal refuse collectors which began as an unofficial movement in support of a far higher claim than that being pursued by the official unions, became official and ended in a high settlement.[6]

The return of the Conservatives

In 1970, for the first time, at least since the war, industrial relations figured as a prominent general-election issue. The unpopularity of incomes policy, the evidence that pay claims and strikes were out of control, the government's capitulation to the unions over the Industrial Relations Bill, were all used by the Conservatives, against which Labour offered its renewed belief in what remained of the post-war consensus. What part these issues played in the outcome it is difficult to determine, but the Conservatives, committed to radical changes in, if not an ending of, the consensus, emerged victorious. They proceeded to implement the policies outlined earlier. These included allowing unemployment to rise, 'standing firm' against public-sector pay claims, and preparing a detailed Industrial Relations Bill. Less tangibly, but at least as important, they cut off many of the accustomed channels of communication between government and unions: the TUC's 1969 policy of intervening in disputes was ignored; the Department of Employment's conciliation machinery was rarely offered during disputes; and the consultation offered to the unions over the Industrial Relations Bill was reduced to the details. The TUC which, on the election of the Conservatives, had repeated its 1951 offer of co-operation to a Tory government, was aggrieved at this curtailment of its accustomed role and rejected any consultation over the Bill.

The major union leaderships were now almost totally estranged from the government, apart from the continuing degree of caution enjoined by the unions' commitment to existing constitutional institutions and social peace, while the government had virtually no interest in reaching compromises. All this was added to the growing shop-floor militancy discernible since 1968: the spread of militancy to new groups, the pay explosion, and also a growing rate of unionization. The number of conflicts rose, and so did the overall number of days lost through strikes. A change in the pattern of conflict was emerging: the number of long, unofficial strikes, particularly in the public sector, rose.[7] This was, of course, a direct result of the government's strategy towards this sector. In the years 1970-2 there were strikes or similar actions among local government manual workers, electricity workers (twice), Post Office employees, health service manual staffs, coal miners and railwaymen, as well as prolonged private-sector disputes in the docks, the building industry and the Ford Motor Company. In three cases – electricity in 1971, mines and docks in 1972 – these led to the declaration of a State of Emergency by the government (previously a rare event in Britain). Totally abandoning the conciliation policy, Ministers politicized several of these disputes by publicly condemning the strikers and occasionally calling on the public to make their feelings known. On one occasion, during an electricity dispute which had led to widescale power cuts, there were a few acts of public violence against electricity workers.

The prolonged nature of the strikes led to workers developing new tactics to strengthen their action. In 1972 the miners developed mass picketing – the deployment of vast numbers of men sufficient to prevent the passage of lorries – outside gas and electricity stations to prevent the use of existing coal stocks or alternative fuels. Later in the same year, building workers used 'flying pickets' (groups of men moving from site to site to prevent the use of black-leg labour), and there were several violent incidents between the pickets and men continuing to work. One such incident, at Shrewsbury, led to the jailing of two strikers who then became a *cause célèbre* as the TUC made official representations on their behalf, and militants organized demonstrations and token actions over the succeeding three years.

In most of these cases the government was forced to climb down in one way or another. The postmen, who entered their dispute ill prepared for a long struggle, were the only major group to be decisively 'beaten' by the government. On some occasions Ministers were forced to accept, against their policy, arbitration or courts of inquiry – the actual verdict of one of these being condemned by the Prime Minister, showing how wide had become the rift between government policy and the mediatory institutions and practices of the post-war consensus. On other occasions, the government itself made massive concessions at the last moment, notably during the miners' strike in 1972, when industry ground to a halt under the impact of power cuts.

Superimposed on and interleaved among all these disputes was the conflict over the Industrial Relations Bill. Its major provisions were based on the themes which had figured in the debates before the Donovan Commission.[8] The main controversial items were the following: henceforth the only unions which could enjoy existing legal immunities (together with certain new positive rights) would be those which had registered with a new Registrar of Trade Unions. To be accepted on to the register, unions would have to incorporate certain provisions into their rules. Some of these concerned purely internal matters, but also included were rules for the powers and duties of all officers, and a clear indication of the union's procedure for calling strikes – including disciplinary measures which a union would have to take against members striking in breach of these provisions. An unregistered union would be free from some, though by no means all, these requirements, but would lose tax concessions on income related to its charitable activities and certain immunities against legal action in the case of trade disputes, and would be excluded from the new legal rights being extended to registered unions and their members (e.g. to act as sole bargaining agent for a group of workers, and to require an employer to recognize the union) The closed shop would also be illegal, though registered unions had the right to something similar. Both registered and unregistered unions had imposed on them a duty to restrain their members from taking industrial action against a legally binding agreement. Legally binding agreements had been unknown in British collective bargaining, but the Bill made it possible for them to be introduced if both or *either* (presumably the employer) of the parties to an agreement so insisted. Since the government wished to avoid the intractable problems of taking large numbers of strikers to court, it was provided that the legal action in the case of breaches of such provisions would be against the union of which the strikers were members, for not preventing their actions. Two additional provisions which survived from Labour's 1969 Bill were for strike ballots and conciliation pauses.

Against these measures which would make the exercise of union and worker power more difficult were improvements in certain rights of both. Some of these can be seen as 'sweeteners', to smooth acceptance of the Bill; others were, as mentioned, extended to registered unions alone and thus acted as an inducement to register; while yet others removed certain issues from conflict within industry and placed them in the law courts. Many of the Bill's provisions took the form of rendering certain kinds of conduct of unions and employers as 'unfair industrial practices' – a new class of legal offence. Accompanying the new offences went an entire new court, the National Industrial Relations Court, which would be a new division of the High Court and would be responsible for the new Act. As a further inducement to the unions to accept the measures, the existing industrial tribunals, which dealt with a mass of questions of workers' rights important to unions and workers alike, were incorporated as part of the mechanism of the new court.

An almost total change in the legal structure of British industrial relations was thus being introduced. Something, however, remained of the voluntarist tradition, and this was an innovation on the policies the Tories had worked out while in opposition. The Commission on Industrial Relations – a body proposed by Donovan and established by Labour in 1969 – would be retained to do its conciliatory and investigatory work on industrial relations problems, and in many cases the Bill provided that an attempt to resolve disputes coming within the terms of the new measure should first be made through its machinery. Alongside the Bill, the government also introduced a Code of Industrial Relations Practice which, while not part of the statute, could be quoted in court: it embodied most of the principles of traditional compromise bargaining.

The government tolerated few amendments to its Bill.[9] Even the CBI, which was beginning to have second thoughts about the new element of legalism which would enter relations between workers and employers, met with a scant response. The TUC, which rejected consultation over detail alone, was faced with a major problem. Acceptance of the Act, meaning essentially the acceptance of registration, would hamstring the unions in nearly all their activities and throw their work into an entirely new and unfamiliar context deliberately designed to reduce their capacity to make demands. On the other hand, rejection meant the loss of tax concessions, the illegality of the closed shop, vulnerability to the poaching of members by any organizations which did register, loss of access to the industrial tribunals and vulnerability to a whole new range of legal offences through the loss of traditional immunities. It was, however, this latter path which the minority of TUC unions chose. A small minority favoured co-operation to secure the best terms possible; a larger majority wanted a more radical policy of opposition, to include strikes and demonstrations. The majority, which prevailed, favoured a policy of passive non-co-operation, but the more radical minority remained active. In December 1970 about half a million workers in the motor and printing industries struck for one day in protest at the Bill, and in March some unions, including the AUEW, supported a further strike by nearly two million workers. Political strikes not counting in Britain as industrial disputes, these do not appear in the strike statistics for those years, which already registered extremely high strike totals. Within parliament, while the government's majority was secure, several left-wing Labour MPs felt they should make a symbolic gesture to indicate the depth of their opposition to the Bill and express solidarity with the unions: they created rowdy scenes and forced many divisions.[10] The official opposition, on the other hand, led by Harold Wilson and Barbara Castle, stressed the instability that would result from the Bill's use of penal sanctions and the scope for creating 'martyrs'; Harold Wilson called the Bill a 'militants' charter' – the authentic voice of the original post-war consensus.

Events following the final passing of the Bill in August 1971 largely concern three developments: the TUC's campaign of continued resistance; the government's own use of the Act; and controversy surrounding the NIRC. In the first of these, the TUC had considerable difficulty holding the line. The policy of non-recognition of the Court was proving expensive for certain unions, especially the TGWU and AUEW which had incurred massive fines for contempt of court by refusing to abide by the Court's orders. Most unions did not flinch in their opposition to the Act, but a few had started to register. These included some who placed a high priority on maintaining the closed shop, such as actors and seamen. Others were caught by a skilful device of the government which had so worded the registration provisions that unions had to vote positively to de-register: some union conferences refused to do this. The registered unions, including some (in the white-collar area) outside the TUC, were now well poised to use the Act's provisions to seek bargaining rights at the expense of non-registered unions. To limit the possibilities of this, the TUC decided in 1972, despite considerable internal division, to expel from membership those unions which had registered. It remained questionable just how long the TUC's policy of passive resistance could last, given the loss of tax concessions and the other problems mentioned here.

But nearly all the unions' difficulties concerned the conflict around the Act as such. They did not have problems from large numbers of employers taking advantage of the new powers it gave them to reduce the scope for industrial action. By far the great majority of employers preferred to retain the relations they had established with the unions; they certainly did not want to provoke new conflict.[11] They made few attempts at introducing legally enforceable agreements or trying to dispose of closed-shop arrangements. Most of the cases to come before the Court concerned very small employers, or individual workers who refused to join unions in closed shops and insisted on taking legal action to the embarrassment of the employers and, at times, the NIRC itself. Two of these cases were, however, highly significant in that the union involved in both, the AUEW, refused to recognize the Court, with the result that colossal damages were awarded against it, including the sequestration of its property.

Another major incident concerned action by dock workers against a transport firm. The incident was part of a more general struggle by dock workers against the establishment of inland container ports. These ports, being outside the geographical limits of the Dock Labour Scheme, were beyond union control. Both the dockers and the road transport drivers at the container depot were members of the TGWU but, given the role of the union in joint regulation with the employers of dock labour, the dockers were far more powerfully organized within the union. In an unofficial action dockers picketed a container firm, Heaton's Transport. Five of the leaders were taken to court by the firm under the Industrial Relations Act. They refused to appear before the NIRC and were duly arrested for contempt. There was immediately a total walk-out on the London docks and, with the five arrested men still refusing to recognize the Court, there was every likelihood of a prolonged and damaging dispute. In a famous episode, the government's Official Solicitor appeared in Court and secured the men's release.

This represented a major climb-down by the government and somewhat justified Harold Wilson's claims about the scope for martyrdom which the Act provided – scope which the government believed it had closed in its provisions for making *unions* rather than individual workers liable to legal action. However, where a case like that of Heaton's was concerned, such a liability would only be incurred by a registered union; in framing the Bill the government had assumed that virtually all unions would eventually register. The law courts then came to the government's rescue: the Heaton's case progressed to the House of Lords, where it was ruled (under Common Law, not the Act) that a union was always responsible for the actions of its shop stewards and therefore the TGWU was liable for the action against Heaton's. Massive fines were imposed.

If the government wanted to create difficulties for trade unions, the Act was working encouragingly. But its more important objectives were not being achieved. The Conservatives had believed that, by exchanging industrial relations law reform for incomes policy, they would not only more effectively limit union power and make strikes more difficult, but would depoliticize industrial relations:

disputes which could not be resolved by the parties would go to the courts, the non-political, neutral courts of English law, and not enter politics. On all these points the Conservatives were utterly wrong. The Act had virtually no impact on mainstream collective bargaining; it actually led to rather than prevented strikes; and the NIRC never became detached from its controversial partisan origins to take its place as an established court of law. The NIRC had originally been instituted as a special court because of powerful arguments that the orthodox machinery of law could not cope with the intricacies of industrial relations – employers' and (but for the boycott by all major unions) union representatives were to sit with judges on the Court. But that very device contributed to the NIRC's lack of legitimacy. It was not regarded as a 'proper' court.

Finally, there is the government's own use of the Act to consider. While, to the annoyance of the CBI, the general tenor of the Act was to place the employers in the front line of litigation against unions, certain powers were reserved to the government, principally those of calling for strike ballots and cooling-off periods in the case of major disputes. (Insofar as the government was itself an employer, it made no use of the Act; both it and the nationalized industries continued, iike most private employers, with industrial relations practices unregulated by law.) During the national railway work-to-rule of 1972 the Secretary of State for Employment, Robert Carr, ordered a conciliation pause and a ballot. The unions complied with the law; the ballot resulted in a colossal majority for action; the work-to-rule resumed as soon as the cooling-off period ended; and the dispute was finally ended in the conventional way.

Perhaps these were all 'teething troubles'; perhaps if the Act had remained in operation for years it would eventually have begun to 'bite'. It was certainly widely believed that the unions were holding on in the expectation of the return of Labour at the next election, which would have to be held by 1975, and that if that did not occur they would have to reconsider their policy. But towards the end of 1972 a development occurred which led the Conservative government away from its earlier hopes for the Act. For a variety of reasons, among which industrial relations was included, the government was having severe economic difficulties. There was a previously unknown combination of high unemployment and high inflation (stagflation as it has become known), the latter being made worse by a rising level of international commodity prices.

Several major companies were faced with grave problems of survival. The government had taken office with the intention of not rushing to the rescue of firms which could not survive market competition. This resolve weakened at the prospect of large increases in unemployment and industrial dislocation. During 1972 a Conservative government thus found itself nationalizing, of all things, Rolls-Royce. Later the same year, an important shipbuilding firm, Upper Clyde Shipbuilders, was scheduled to close down. The redundant workers staged a sit-down strike in the works which lasted for several weeks (becoming a work-in) until the government helped negotiate a take-over by an American company. The UCS work-in became a signal and example for workers faced with plant closure, not only in Britain but throughout Europe. There were many similar examples in the following years, several of them becoming, at least temporarily, workers' co-operatives.

The government made a dramatic shift in its economic policies. Instead of the public-spending cuts and tight money policy of its first two years, it launched a massive increase in public spending without tax increases (leading to a major increase in the money supply) in an attempt at engineering economic expansion. In place of its previous policy of reducing state intervention in industry, it introduced a highly interventionist Industry Act. And in place of its avoidance of dealings with the unions and of incomes policy, it launched a series of tripartite talks between Ministers, the CBI and the TUC in an attempt to reach agreement on overall economic policy – including prices and incomes restraint.

It was a return to the policies of the 1960s, though in more difficult economic circumstances. It was not really an attempt at returning to the post-war consensus: that had rested on highly implicit agreements and fortuitous circumstances. Since 1961, attempts at refurbishing a national-level agreement had needed to be more explicit, more based on formal institutions, leading gradually to a total change in the character of the system. Now the scope for consensus – in the context of the rising power of shop-floor militancy, the political strength which the unions had discovered since 1969, and the radical breach between the Conservatives and the unions since 1970 – was very remote indeed. In particular, the tricky task of producing a national political-level structure without politicization was now impossible although, as we shall see, the process of tacit mutual adjustment between government and unions had not entirely vanished.

The return and demise of incomes policy

The Prime Minister, Edward Heath, said he was inviting the two sides of industry to share in the formulation of economic policy in exchange for restraint, and the unions responded by raising demands across the whole area of policy – including, of course, repeal of the Industrial Relations Act. Mr Heath could not accept this interpretation of his invitation and the talks were dead-locked; however, it is notable that from that time onwards the government itself made no further use of the Act.

Agreement could not be reached on incomes policy: the unions wanted tighter price controls than the government and the CBI were prepared to contemplate, and the government would only consider such measures if there were statutory pay controls. The government broke off the talks and introduced an entirely statutory pay and prices policy with far tougher sanctions than anything under the Labour government. The first stage was a statutory three-month freeze. This was followed by a more elaborate stage two.

A national norm was established and legally enforced. This specified the average level of increase which could be awarded to any group of workers, collective bargaining being allowed to determine distribution within the group. The norm comprised a flat-rate as well as the usual percentage element and a ceiling on the overall sum that any individual could receive – steps towards redistribution in favour of the low paid. A Pay Board was established to monitor the policy (paralleled by a Price Commission on the prices side). This did not carry out detailed investigations as the NBPI had done, but undertook the technical and legal task of ensuring that the norm, with its limited exceptions, was upheld. In case of a breach of the pay code, the Board would issue a warning notice followed, if necessary, by an order prohibiting the increase. The Board exercised these powers itself, and although the Secretary of State for Employment retained an ultimate right to use his discretion to intervene, the system was designed to operate without continual activity at the political level – in contrast to the NBPI. It is notable, given the poor state of relations between government and unions, and given the lengths to which the unions had gone to oppose the Industrial Relations Act and the NIRC, that few warning notices and very few restraining orders were issued, and there were no strikes against the use of orders.

A further, and perhaps more significant, sanction consisted of a link between the pay code and the statutory prices code : a company could not claim, among its grounds for seeking to raise a price, the fact that it had had to concede a pay claim going beyond the pay code.

Stage two of the policy was followed by a third stage which incorporated a different norm and other changes,

notably threshold agreements. This was a device advocated by the TUC whereby pay would be automatically
augmented if the retail price index rose by more than a
certain percentage over a certain period. In setting the
levels for operation of the thresholds, the government was
confident that they would hardly be used, but would give
workers confidence that their pay settlements would not be
eroded by inflation. In fact, however, the period of operation of the threshold, which outlasted the Conservative
government, saw the most rapid rise in inflation in modern
British history.

It has been noted that the unions posed no real challenge to the legal operation of the policy, and it was remarkably effective in restraining incomes for most of
1973. At the collective bargaining stage, however, there
continued to be large strikes, especially in the public
sector. Further, against the advice of its General Council,
the TUC called for a national 'day of action' in protest
against stage three of the policy. This was widely interpreted as meaning a day of strikes, though the General
Council tried to play this down. The period was certainly
one of intensified conflict and bitterness; but the policy
was relatively successful, wages increasing by little more
than the norm throughout stage two and for much of
stage three, though it should be remembered that the time
period concerned was little more than a year. Overall,
however, the economic situation was not encouraging.
Inflation, resulting largely from commodity price rises, continued; after the floating of the pound sterling in 1972 the
currency continued to decline sharply; and the tough price
controls were exacerbating a long-term decline in the rate
of profit, leading to a reduction of investment.

Then, in autumn 1973, came the Middle East war and
the large increase in the price of oil subsequently
engineered by the Arab countries. This was bound to, and
did, create enormous problems for all Western nations
for several years; for Britain it also provoked a major
political crisis. Among the groups whose pay claims were

looming in late 1973 were the electrical power engineers, the railwaymen and the coal miners – all seeking rises in excess of the norm and all capable of wielding considerable industrial strength. The miners had already humiliated the government in 1972. In anticipation of difficulty, the government had concocted criteria for exceptional rises at stage three, designed almost specifically to give the miners a large increase within the terms of the policy. But the oil crisis threw all these calculations into confusion: suddenly the labour-market position of all workers in industries competing with oil was considerably strengthened – and this included all three of the groups mentioned. The miners' case was particularly important, since for years coal had been declining, in the shadow of the great rise in the use of oil, a much cheaper fuel. All this was now changing rapidly.

As is well known, the National Union of Mineworkers refused to reach an agreement within the incomes policy, and imposed an overtime ban, the effects of which were soon felt on industrial activity. The government had no intention of giving way and in December imposed large-scale power cuts and reduced industry to a three-day working week in order to conserve coal supplies. The NUM responded to this by calling a full-scale strike. Several interests associated with the Conservative Party began to urge Edward Heath to call a general election on the issue, 'Who governs Britain: the unions or the government?' Such a line was a logical development of the policy, noted above, of trying to use public opinion against strikers. At first he demurred but, despite a flurry of activity, there was no progress in reconciling the dispute, while opinion polls were suggesting considerable support for the government's stand. Mr Heath finally called an election for 28 February 1974, and there began the only election campaign in British history in which industrial relations, only twenty years previously the great unmentionable in partisan conflict, were the central issue in a bitter campaign. It was also the most polarized election of recent times.

However, the final result showed neither public acceptance of that polarization nor the sweeping majority for the Conservatives which had been so widely predicted. There was unprecedented success for the minor parties — the Liberals, Scottish and Welsh Nationalists and Ulster Unionists — and while the Conservatives secured a slightly bigger share of the popular vote than Labour, the latter secured more seats and, after a few days during which Mr Heath tried unsuccessfully to form a coalition with the Liberals, became the governing party.[12]

The February 1974 election was obviously an event of major importance to any study of the politics of industrial relations, though its significance has, in my view, been widely misinterpreted, being popularly regarded as the occasion when 'the miners brought down the government'. As I have written elsewhere:[13]

As this phrase passes into history it leaves the impression of a government which found it impossible to continue and abdicated its office when confronted with a power challenge which it could not face. Retrospectively, the election of February 1974 does seem to bear out such an interpretation; after all, the Conservatives did leave office. However, to leave the account there is to ignore completely the political context in January and February 1974. Irrespective of the mining dispute, the energy crisis had . . . dealt a severe blow to Stage 3 policy. The threshold agreement alone was certain to introduce an unforeseen element of wage inflation. Further, some time between the following autumn and the spring of 1975 the government would want to hold a general election. The prospects for its popularity by that period were not good. However, it appeared from public opinion polls that the government could call on considerable public support in its firm stand against the miners. If it went to the country on the issue . . . it could expect a much-increased majority, be free of electioneering until 1978 and thus hold the line against the miners and any subsequent challenges. Certainly the voices in the press and the Conservative Party which urged the Prime Minister to go to the country from December 1973 onwards were not the voices of despair urging abdication, but those wanting a Conservative administration to capitalize on what was believed to be a widespread public loathing of trade unions.

What the election did show was: that yet another central pillar of the post-war consensus – the avoidance of the politicization of industrial conflict – had finally crumbled as the preferred policy of a Conservative government; that, however, it was far from clear whether the opposite policy – trying to capitalize on the fact that industrial unrest tended to be blamed on to the Labour movement – had much promise; and that, faced with such a politicization, the British electorate did not, as earlier generations of Conservatives had feared, rush to the barricades, but spurned *both* parties associated with the conflict. In a curious way it was the post-war consensus which 'won' the February 1974 election, even though that victory was registered in the votes of the minor parties which historically had had little to do with it.

Chapter 4

Picking up the Pieces
(since 1974)

The title of this chapter is not intended to imply that there was a sudden end to the developments of the preceding decade after the February election. As will be seen below, in several respects certain processes of change continued unabated while others did so after a brief interruption. There was, however, under the new Labour government a renewed attempt at building a national consensus, albeit on different terms and less successfully than that of the 1940s. The government, indeed, formally called its policy the 'social contract'.

During its period in opposition, Labour had placed great stress on rebuilding its badly damaged relations with the unions. From late 1972 onwards, this became crystallized in a series of talks between the national executive committee of the party and the General Council of the TUC. It is more than coincidence that the talks took place at the same time as – and covered similar ground to – the series of discussions being conducted between the Conservative government, the TUC and the CBI. It had become clear to all involved, irrespective of party, that in future a far greater degree of explicit consultation would be necessary on overall economic policy between government and the major industrial interest groups. For obvious reasons – including its being in opposition, as well as its special party-union links – Labour's talks had made more progress than those of the Conservatives. The Labour Party leaders had agreed – not entirely eagerly – to repeal the Industrial Relations Act and the statutory incomes policy; to strengthen price controls; to introduce legislation strengthening union and worker rights; to introduce industrial democracy; and to pursue certain agreed social and economic policies. In exchange, the unions would voluntarily recognize the need to take the overall position of the economy into account when making wage claims.

During the February 1974 general election campaign, when Labour was pressed to state with what it would replace the Conservatives' incomes policy, this agreement with the unions was promoted in importance to become the social contract on which the party's approach would be founded, and such it became after the election. The Tories' stage three incomes policy was not immediately scrapped but ran its course, though the Secretary of State for Employment, Michael Foot, was prepared to use his discretionary powers under it to allow certain settlements above the norm. In many respects the Department of Employment temporarily returned to its old role, pursuing conciliation at almost any cost. Thereafter income restraint took the form of attempts by the TUC to moderate claims. This was an intensely difficult period for anyone attempting income restraint. The international wave of price increases in the wake of oil and other commodity price rises produced enormous increases in the cost of living for which people tried to compensate through increased pay. The size of claims, the number of strikes and the proportion of the work-force joining trade unions all continued to grow as they had done throughout the 1970s. Meanwhile, the thresholds of the existing stage three were triggered with increasing frequency, providing automatic large rises for all those who had negotiated threshold arrangements.

While many of the important developments during the life of this Labour government concern the reappearance of incomes policy, there were also major changes in labour law. The Trade Union and Labour Relations Act 1974 repealed the Industrial Relations Act and introduced various changes which strengthened the power of unions. However, the government's difficulty in sustaining a majority in the Commons and the heavily anti-Labour majority in the Lords resulted in several opposition amendments emasculating the Bill. For several months there was continual parliamentary excitement as the government kept introducing legislation which the opposition frustrated. Conservative peers threatened a constitutional crisis between Lords and Commons and put their trust in the supposed public unpopularity of unions to prevent Labour taking advantage of the presumed power of an appeal to public opinion on behalf of elected democracy against a House of hereditary and appointed origins. Eventually the Employment Protection Act 1975 and the Trade Union and Labour Relations (Amendment) Act 1976 introduced the government's full policy.

The main conflict over the Bills centred on the Conservatives' attempt at protecting the rights of workers who refused to join trade unions in firms where unions had managed to obtain a closed shop. Particular concern was expressed over the possibility that there might be a closed shop among journalists in the newspaper industry, which it was felt threatened the power of proprietors to control the press (a power generally referred to as the 'freedom of the press'). Michael Foot, Secretary of State for Employment, eventually negotiated the unusual device of a charter on industrial relations in the newspaper industry, which, while having no statutory force, was incorporated into the Act. While this conflict attracted more public political attention than virtually anything else in the Bills, it is doubtful whether it should loom so large in any historical perspective. As I have written elsewhere:[1]

The extraordinary fact about this issue is that although the legislation repealed the ban on the closed shop which had been imposed by the 1971 Act, it did little more than return to the situation which had obtained for many years before 1971; and in any case . . . there is evidence that those provisions of the Industrial Relations Act had made little impact on the practice within industry. Further, the Government's policy involved nothing specific on the newspaper industry at all. In that and in all other sectors the position remains as it had been before 1971 (and the practice as it had been in the 1971-4 period): a closed shop could be introduced only if an employer conceded it in bargaining. What the new legislation did do was to leave dismissal for non-membership of a trade union where a closed-shop agreement existed among the reasons for which an employee could be dismissed . . ., within a law which otherwise extended the individual's freedoms (a) to join a trade union and (b) from unfair dismissal by his employer.

Overall, these Acts represented a highly important extension in the rights of workers and, even more so, of trade unions, with very little conceded directly to employers in exchange. The legislation clearly shifted the balance of power within industrial relations, and employers, the press, Conservatives and – to a certain extent – the judiciary have continued to display towards these Acts an intermittent hostility falling short of outright opposition. Some might argue that within the social contract the government's main aim was to make possible an agreement on wage restraint. More subtly, it could also be claimed that one net effect of the legislation has been to make British unions for the first time in history more dependent on state-given legal rights than on their own autonomous power. There is substance in both these points, but they do not detract from the extensions of rights embodied in the Acts.

Individual workers secured: considerable protection against dismissal (going some way beyond the protection first introduced in the 1971 Act, it should however be noted); improved redundancy arrangements; paid time off from work to carry out union duties, and (for women workers) paid maternity leave. Unions gained: a legal procedure for securing a right to recognition; a further extension of immunities from Common Law actions, in the century-old struggle between parliament and the law courts over the definition of a trade dispute: improved arbitration facilities through a new body, the Advisory, Conciliation and

Arbitration Service; and new rights of access to information relevant to bargaining.

In trying to assess the implications of all this for industrial relations, it is important to note that British unions have for the first time placed their faith in legal and state-sponsored organizations for securing their rights and powers. This represents a tremendous shift in position since the mid-1960s when they argued so strenuously before Donovan for a highly voluntarist system. The change probably reflects three things: the unions' new confidence – after the conflict over the Industrial Relations Bill 1969, the Industrial Relations Act 1971, and the mining dispute of 1973-4 – that they can overcome attempts at using state power against them, and that they run less risk than they used to believe of getting the worst of legal intervention; their realization that complete state abstention from industrial relations has become a thing of the past and that they should instead try to ensure that the inevitable involvement would serve their own interests; and, perhaps most important, their uniquely powerful political position after the events of 1969 and 1972-4. All the same, the unions are still not without misgivings over the new system. They have made considerable use of their new rights but are dubious about the legal entanglements which it threatens.

It should be noted that much of the non-legal conciliation tradition has survived in the structure and practice of ACAS. The service has its origins in the early 1970s, when the TUC and, with less enthusiasm, the CBI, after the discrediting of the DE's services under the Conservative government, had talks about setting up a private conciliation service. ACAS itself is not part of the government machinery, the Secretary of State appointing its members from among representatives of the TUC and the CBI together with certain 'independent' academics. Its first chairman, Jim Mortimer, is a former trade-union officer (of the draughtsmen's union) *and* former labour relations director for London Transport. ACAS operates largely on a voluntarist conciliation basis, and also appoints the members of an independent Central Arbitration Committee. This carries out arbitration work on the traditional pattern, though in the case of union claims for recognition it is able to make legally binding decisions. Tribunals operating under the ACAS umbrella decide cases which affect the wide range of rights established by the new employment legislation. It is not possible, without elaborate research into case decisions, to draw any detailed conclusions from its patterns and directions of activity, but one prominent and sometimes controversial area concerns claims for union recognition – either claims by workers against an employer who refuses to accept a union, or competing claims between two or more unions. (One notorious example is the Grunwick dispute, discussed on pages 113ff.) An important guiding principle for ACAS is that of 'good industrial relations', which means, broadly, that union recognition is a good thing and that existing, established unions, especially those already present within a firm, should have priority over newcomers. At present this latter criterion is mainly being used to ensure that TUC-affiliated unions are able to keep outsiders at bay – particularly relevant in that most cases of new unionization now concern white-collar employees, among whom professional associations not linked to the main union movement are active.

Finally, it is significant that ACAS has a tripartite system of control. This system has been paralleled elsewhere in recent years: a tripartite Health and Safety Commission has replaced the DE's responsibilities in that area, while a tripartite Manpower Services Commission has taken over industrial training, the operation of employment exchanges and policies for alleviating unemployment. This shift can be seen as part of the move, developing since the war but intensified in the 1970s, towards involving unions and employer organizations in the conduct of industrial policy. It also marks the final decline of the old Ministry of Labour, which formerly carried out all those functions, and which could only operate so long as it made sense to have a Ministry acting partly outside the general ambit of government policy in which employer and employee interests alike could put trust.

The reappearance of incomes policy

Although Labour accepted flexibility in its inherited and soon-to-be-abolished pay policy, it maintained a strict regime on prices. Many firms, caught between restrained prices and high wage claims, experienced crises of profitability, made worse by the effect on output of the three-day week and the general recession afflicting Western economies, largely though not entirely as a result of the oil crisis. There was an increase in bankruptcies and redundancies. The policy which Labour developed to meet these problems consisted of measures of state involvement, sometimes including but more often short of outright nationalization. This was largely the responsibility of the Department of Industry, the Secretary of State for which was Tony Benn, who, during the period in opposition, had become a leader of Labour's left wing. On several occasions his department tried to help workers in threatened firms to establish workers' co-operatives. A general mood of panic and alarm spread through British industry, the political right and, more immediately important, the overseas holders of sterling – though in October 1974 Labour was able to hold a general election in which it improved its parliamentary position, albeit by a small margin.

It became clear that matters could not continue indefinitely as they were. Policies of Tony Benn's kind could not be maintained unless accompanied by further steps to insulate the economy from international pressures; and, whether this strategy or a more orthodox one were pursued, the rising rate of incomes would need attention. After the experience of the preceding decade, however, it was inconceivable that any move on incomes policy could be made without the agreement of the unions.

In July 1975 the government held its promised referendum on Britain's membership of the European Economic Community. The majority of the cabinet, most Conservatives, the Liberals and the CBI backed continued membership; the TUC, the Labour left – largely under the leadership of Tony Benn – and some right-wing Conservative groups advocated withdrawal. The result, a substantial majority for continued membership, meant that the left and the unions suffered a set-back in terms of public support. Shortly afterwards, Benn was moved to a different department, and his successor, Eric Varley, pursued a far more orthodox policy towards state intervention and co-operatives. This automatically increased the government's dependence on the private sector for economic recovery. The CBI, which had hitherto been a less full participant in the tripartite structure, began to have more opportunities for pressing on government its policy preferences.

However, in the first fruits of the new orientation the unions still held the initiative. There were rumours that the government was thinking of a more explicit and formal, but still voluntary, incomes policy. Jack Jones, General Secretary of the TGWU, made a speech advocating something of the same kind. Mr Jones, originally a dominant figure among the new radical union leaderships which had made life difficult for the Conservative and preceding Labour governments, was now a dedicated supporter of the Labour administration. A major architect of the social contract, he valued the new accord between party and unions, saw enormous scope for securing the unions' political and social goals through this channel, and was determined not to see a Conservative government return to destroy the achievements. His support, and hence that of the TGWU, was now assured for the government. Shortly afterwards, the TUC proposed a package consisting primarily of: a commitment to reduce inflation at a certain rate; continued price controls; a flat-rate pay increase for the next year; and no pay rises at all for those on high incomes. With minor amendments, this policy was agreed by the government and the CBI and incorporated in a White Paper, *The Attack on Inflation*,[2] which warned of dire consequences if there were no wage restraint.

The following spring the government made overtures to the TUC for a policy to replace the initial agreement later that year. In an unprecedented step the Chancellor of the Exchequer, Denis Healey, announced in his Budget speech that reductions in income tax could be introduced if a satisfactory agreement on wage restraint were reached with the unions. This caused a minor flurry of controversy on the grounds that the unions were in effect being allowed to legislate on tax rates. This was an exaggeration. The behaviour of wage rates during the year would obviously be relevant to the government's fiscal regulation of demand. What the Chancellor was doing was making this process open to explicit discussion rather than leaving it to a kind of 'blind-man's buff' whereby tax changes and wage rises tried to compensate for one another during the year. But the opening of the question to explicit debate was significant in further developing the policy, started by Edward Heath, of engaging the TUC and CBI in economic policy discussions in order to forge a consensus on income restraint.

This point needs careful interpretation. It does not necessarily mean that the unions had secured a new power to determine government policy. The government was able to a large extent to control the policy agenda which it would discuss with the unions, and this control could be used in order to gain the initiative in the tripartite talks. Mr Heath had done something similar when he invited the TUC and CBI to discuss a rather selective list of policy areas. Denis Healey was now seizing the initiative much more squarely by, in effect, challenging the unions either to accept wage restraint or to have higher tax payments imposed both on their members and on everybody else.

A final important point, highlighted by this small but significant step of the Chancellor, is the inter-relation between tax rates and pay rises. Research carried out by Wilkinson and Turner[3] on the wage explosions of 1969 and the early 1970s suggested that the big pay claims of those years reflected, in part, workers' attempts to recoup through wage bargaining the income they had lost through previous large tax increases. It was only from the mid-1960s that income tax began noticeably to erode the wages of the bulk of the manual workers – especially after the Budget of 1969 which abolished the lower rates of tax leading up to the standard rate. By the mid-1970s this had become a more explicit bargaining process – union leaders would quote taxation increases as grounds for pay rises. When, in 1975, Mr Healey began to threaten that excessive pay increases may have to be recouped through increases in income tax, the prospect of a competitive vicious spiral of tax and wage changes loomed ominously. Mr Healey's successful attempt in 1976 to take advantage of the government's new agreement with the unions to exchange tax cuts for wage restraint also forced a benign change of direction on the spiral. All this shows another way in which industrial relations were becoming irretrievably politicized: the growing scale of taxation led to a struggle over fiscal distribution becoming part of the existing wage struggle.

The unions accepted a phase two of the policy, on slightly amended terms. In particular, the TUC was concerned about the erosion of differentials which had taken place as a result of the mildly egalitarian element in the incomes policies of both the Conservative and Labour governments. Partly this reflected the traditional concerns of skilled manual workers, powerfully represented within the TUC. But it was also a sign of the growing role of white-collar unions.[4] Since the late 1960s, union membership among white-collar workers had expanded as more of these workers came to see unionization as a means of joining the pursuit of higher pay, helped from 1974 onwards by greater legal rights to union recognition where employers had resisted it. Further, several white-collar unions which had stood outside the TUC became affiliated.

These two phases of the incomes policy were remarkably successful. Not only did pay rises stay broadly in line with the policy, but the number of strikes, including unofficial ones, dropped from the colossal levels of the early 1970s right back to those of earlier years. Several reasons can be adduced for this dramatic shift, though it would require detailed research to corroborate them and assess their relative importance. There were the straightforward sanctions wielded by the government: its rigid adherence to the policy within the public sector and the use of its growing network of industrial intervention to require private firms to comply. This certainly stiffened the resolve of employers to resist claims, but such a resolve by itself would almost certainly have provoked a rise in the number and duration of strikes aimed at breaking employer resistance; therefore this cannot in itself be the full explanation.

A very important factor was the wholehearted support of the TUC for the policy. The TUC had over the years grown vastly in importance from being a loose co-ordinating centre to being a central channel between unions and government – at a time when the role of government was constantly increasing. It was therefore of considerable importance to any individual union to retain the goodwill of the Congress as a whole – in effect of its General Council – otherwise a range of organizational sanctions could be brought into play against it. This factor played a part in defusing several potential threats to the policy, for example from the coal miners, whose albeit divided leadership kept the NUM on a course of compliance with the policy despite tremendous internal pressure for a return to the aggressive tactics of the early 1970s. On one occasion the workings of the subtle network of sanctions became more blatant: the National Union of Seamen planned a strike in breach of the policy and were threatened with expulsion from the TUC. Expulsion would mean being cut off from sharing in communications with government, from participation in the growing web of tripartite organizations and from protection against poaching of members by other unions. The NUS complied with a compromise deal worked out by the TUC.

The strength of the TUC's own commitment to the policy, and also directly that of many unions, was partly conditioned by their desire to preserve the Labour government in office, and this desire was in turn partly due to the personal commitment of individuals such as Jack Jones, Hugh Scanlon, and Joe Gormley and Lawrence Daly, leaders respectively of the TGWU, the AUEW and the NUM – the three most militant unions of the early 1970s. But the reasons for the TUC's commitment extended much further than this. Labour had given the unions, as organizations, a more deeply embedded role in society than they had ever enjoyed before, in terms both of their legal rights to establish themselves within areas of employment, and of their involvement in policy-making and administration. Against all this, in the actual content of overall economic policy the government had, since 1975, drifted even further from the policies of the TUC and was maintaining a level of unemployment which unions regarded as unacceptably high; the possible effect of this on their attitude to the government was, however, offset by the position being adopted by the Conservative opposition.

Following the *débâcle* of 1974 the Conservatives jettisoned Edward Heath and his closest colleagues, the Industrial Relations Act and incomes policy. Under the leadership of Margaret Thatcher and Sir Keith Joseph they turned back, as in the mid-1960s, to a policy of economic *laissez faire*. It is difficult to give a definite account of the party's policies at this time because Mrs Thatcher deliberately avoided making electoral commitments which might embarrass her in office. Thus, a speech by one Tory spokesman implying policies of hostility towards trade unions would be followed after a short interval by one expounding conciliation. However, certain points were fairly clear. The Conservatives were opposed more strongly than they had been for many years to government intervention in the economy. This had two implications of direct importance to the unions: first, the likely dismantling of many tripartite institutions in which they had a direct stake; and second, as an alternative to government intervention, including incomes policy, a Conservative government would have to regulate the economy through policies entailing even higher levels of unemployment. Finally, while no actual policies have been presented on industrial relations, Conservative leaders, particularly Mrs Thatcher, gave such weight in their pronouncements to attacks on the unions (in particular on the closed shop) that the unions had considerable cause for concern about the policies which a Tory government would pursue. All in all, the unions had a strong incentive to keep Labour in power, even if it were at times a case of, in Belloc's words:

> Holding tightly on to nurse
> For fear of meeting something worse.

A further reason strengthening union support, and probably also widespread support by workers, for the incomes policy was a genuine fear for the future. British society was shaken by the intensified social conflict, galloping inflation and rapidly deteriorating economy of the mid-1970s. Since the early 1950s the country had moved from an unquestioned assumption of international superiority to a desperate awareness of an economic decline which now threatened to become even worse. The February 1974 election and the three-day week had given a major thrust to this mood, and the tone of the White Paper *The Attack on Inflation* had ramified it by referring to the threat of the

British people being 'engulfed by a general catastrophe of incalculable proportions'. Workers and their unions were aware that their wage militancy was seen by many as a contributory factor to this crisis.

It is always difficult to assess how much weight to place on 'awareness' of this kind; but in this case subjective awareness had a powerful material support. The level of unemployment and, more dramatically, the incidence of bankruptcy and redundancy, had risen steeply since 1975.[5] But unemployment had been rising, with only intermittent improvements, since the late 1960s – the very period of growing industrial conflict, wage increases and inflation. It follows that there is no simple relationship between unemployment rates and wage militancy, and the other factors discussed here are necessary in order to help explain the decline in militancy from late 1975. There is, however, also some evidence that unemployment was now beginning to 'bite' in a way that it did not in the early 1970s. Unemployment does not necessarily fall equally on all areas of employment. In the early 1970s it fell predominantly on the private services sector of the economy, leaving the more heavily unionized manufacturing and public sectors *relatively* unaffected; by 1975 it was more evenly distributed, a fact highlighted by the closure of an increasing number of manufacturing plants or firms, and by redundancies in the public sector. From late 1975 trade-union bargaining strength was increasingly being deployed to secure generous redundancy terms and favourable lay-off procedures; major examples were the motor and steel industries. The restoration of full employment became the unions' primary goal. In June 1976 the TGWU launched a call for a 35-hour week to ease unemployment – a theme taken up in bargaining by various unions in subsequent years, with some success by the Post Office Engineering Union in 1978. In some of these campaigns unions were able to score considerable success, but their essentially defensive nature makes a strong contrast with the preceding years.

Phase three: the consensus loosens

By 1975 Britain's inflation rate had become the highest in the Western industrial world, and although it was coming down it was doing so more slowly than predicted and more slowly than those of competitor countries. While the government had made major steps in the direction of the new economic orthodoxy of monetarism, it had done too little to relieve the anxieties of overseas holders of sterling. Public spending had been only slightly cut back, and the government had made substantial international borrowings on the strength of its prospective earnings from North Sea oil, in order to cover its deficit. In the autumn of 1976 a sterling crisis of unprecedented dimensions developed. There had been signs that the government and the Bank of England were prepared to let the pound fall in order to improve the price competitiveness of British exports and thereby alleviate the vast deficit in the balance of payments. This led to fear that the rate would continue to fall unimpeded, which in turn led to heavier selling. To make matters worse, the Labour Party's annual conference was in session during the high point of the crisis; delegates were already hostile to the government because of what was seen as its betrayal of the policies on which it was elected. Demands were made for a determined stand against capitalist interests – demands given added point by the behaviour of capital in the foreign exchange markets. All this, of course, created even greater panic among holders of the currency.

Whatever the Labour Party's constitution may say about the role of the annual conference in its policy-making, a galloping collapse on the foreign exchange markets is a somewhat more salient pressure on Labour Ministers than the votes of a party conference, even if they include representatives of the major unions. The government was forced to negotiate international stand-by credit from the International Monetary Fund on humiliating terms. The pursuit of rigid targets on key indicators, especially the money supply, had to be agreed with the Fund, tying the government even more closely to monetarism. Unemployment would have to rise and public spending be reduced heavily. Little remained of Labour's economic policies. Whatever loss of prestige parliament had suffered in 1976 by the negotiation of tax changes with the TUC seems small by comparison with the facts that the Budgets of 1977 had to be cleared in advance with the IMF.

When it came to negotiating a phase three of incomes policy as Mr Healey prepared his Budget early in 1977, the gulf between the government and the TUC on general economic policy had become wide. Further, the previous two years had seen an overall decline in the standard of living of virtually everyone in Britain, while higher-paid workers were resentful at the earlier erosion of their differentials. In several industries a movement of shop stewards was developing in opposition to any renewal of incomes policy. Anxious to avoid difficulties with their members of the kind experienced in 1950 and 1968, union leaders refused to agree to a new round. The TUC called for a return to free collective bargaining, but stressed that this should be 'orderly'. The government insisted on a more formal specification of norms – this time as a percentage (10 per cent), giving larger increases to those on higher incomes – and, in the absence of TUC consent, administered it alone. On one point government and unions remained in agreement: there be an interval of twelve months between pay awards.

During 1977-8 the level of industrial conflict rose. There were some major strikes among bakery workers, air traffic controllers and, most alarmingly, firemen. However, employers' resistance was strong, especially in the public sector. Even in the case of the firemen, the government refused to move and eventually the union, like many others, virtually admitted defeat. The contrast with the 1950s in the role of government in industrial disputes could hardly be more complete. In the private sector the government reinforced its policy through a controversial use of contracts: firms taking on contracts for the government were required to accept a clause committing them *generally* – and any sub-contractors engaged by them – to observe the pay policy. The terms of this were modified following CBI opposition.

The lack of support given by the TUC to phase three did not mean a frontal assault by the unions on income restraint; rather than opposition, the TUC offered the government implicit and general compliance instead of the explicit, detailed support of the two previous years. This seems to be what they meant by an 'orderly' return to free collective bargaining. Unions trying to break the policy were not threatened with sanctions as the NUS had been, but they were not offered support either. Len Murray, General Secretary of the TUC, played a prominent part in mediating and conciliating in disputes such as that in the fire service, but the general direction of his activities seems to have been to lean on the union concerned.

In 1978 the government tried to reach agreement on a phase four, with a percentage norm set even lower at 5 per cent. The rate of inflation had subsided considerably, now running at about 8 per cent, but was still higher than those of most competitor countries. The unions adopted the same position as the previous year and, with Jack Jones retiring from the General Secretaryship of the TGWU, a major bastion of support for the social contract was leaving the scene. But the unions were still tied, if anything more tightly, to their commitment to the Labour government. The unions' dilemma was nicely summarized in two resolutions passed at the Trades Union Congress, one expressing complete support for the Labour government, the other rejecting the incomes policy of the same government. For its part, in deciding to adopt a tough stance, the government took a new and risky weapon to its armoury. During the week of the Congress the Prime Minister, James Callaghan, announced that the general election widely expected to take place in October would not be held until some time later during the following twelve months. This decision put the government's fate very much at the mercy of the unions' bargaining behaviour during the coming winter, but by the same token imposed a new pressure on the unions not to 'rock the boat'. At the time of writing the outcome of this gamble is still to be revealed.

The changing shape of industrial relations

In several respects the British system of industrial relations is unrecognizable from that of the early 1950s. The universal agreement on keeping industrial relations out of politics has become a hopeless aspiration; government commitment to a strategy of mediation and conciliation has gone; so has full employment; domination of the trade-union movement by a highly centralized leadership committed to supporting national policy disintegrated, though it has staged a partial come-back since 1975. The consensus on post-war recovery has also gone, by the early 1970s being replaced by a higher level of dissensus than Britain has seen for many years, although something resembling a consensus on avoiding economic disaster has again developed since 1975.

On the other hand, the detailed integration of trade-union leaderships into the political and economic institution of the country has become much more widespread. The paradox at the heart of the post-war consensus – a growing national political involvement of trade unions alongside a depoliticization of industrial relations – has increasingly been resolved at the expense of the latter.

A further element of continuity is the deep-seated liberalism of industrial relations, shown in the reluctance of all concerned to move away from a model of the two sides of industry confronting each other in bargaining and accommodating their conflicting interests without external regulation. It is a model which has taken a severe battering over the past two decades, and much of Parts Two and Three of this book will be devoted to an analysis of how it has changed and how the emerging new model, if such exists, may be defined. But the tenacity of the old system and the uncertain hold of any replacement is apparent in the persistent failure of any new institutions to take root or, with the exception of the NEDC, to survive changes of government.

In conclusion, two further developments during the past few very eventful years indicate some of these continuing tensions and uncertainties. First, there is the fate of the Bullock Committee of Inquiry on Industrial Democracy appointed by the government in 1975.[6] Support for worker participation in management has always been a minority strand among British unions. The majority has always favoured confrontational bargaining, facing the employers across the table with no confusion of roles or responsibilities. Participation in management has been seen as a trap, disabling unions from representing their members unambiguously if the participation involved the unions, or giving workers a representative channel in rivalry to the unions if they were excluded. On the other side, management had no desire to share information or decision-making with workers. There were therefore few incentives for anyone to raise the issue.

There were slight signs of change in the mid-1960s: unions in the steel industry supported proposals for the appointment of worker-directors after nationalization of the industry – largely a reaction against the total exclusion of workers from any participation in the post-war wave of nationalization, the arguments in the public sector being somewhat different from those in the private. But the experiment was a minor, cautious one and was not widely debated.[7] More significantly, perhaps, the TUC actually advocated participation in management in its written evidence to the Donovan Commission. The passage was entirely ignored at the time – the issue was so far removed from the central concerns of that Commission – and no unions pressed it; it was largely written off as an idiosyncratic whim of the TUC officials who drafted the evidence.

In the early 1970s the issue acquired more substance when the EEC began to prepare a draft EEC company law. Participation has figured more prominently in several EEC countries than in Britain. In West Germany there has been an important system of co-determination in the coal and steel industries, and in nearly all countries there has been a statutory system of works councils which usually by-pass union channels of representation. This was the time when Britain's entry to the Community was being negotiated, and although the majority of unions opposed entry they prepared themselves for its implications. The TUC set out a policy on the form that participation should take if it ever came into being, insisting, against European practice, that there must be 50-per-cent worker membership of company boards, that elections of worker-directors must be conducted through union channels, and that the fact of participation should not impede unions' freedom in collective bargaining.[8]

The policy became more deeply rooted in the TUC's political demands. Of particular importance was the fact that Jack Jones, the main guardian of the social contract, had become an enthusiastic advocate. A pledge to investigate it formed part of the Labour Party's commitment to the unions under the social contract, and was embodied in the party's 1974 election manifestos as a third stage in legislation, the first two being the repeal of the Industrial Relations Act and the new union and employment protection laws. However, rather than move to immediate legislation the Labour government appointed the committee under Lord Bullock.

The change in union policy can be explained on various grounds, in addition to the political needs to confront the

EEC with a home-grown policy and to take note of Jack Jones's preferences. The growing complexity of company financial structure, in particular the role of multi-national corporations, was making it more and more difficult for unions to bargain knowledgeably. Statutory disclosures of information by management to unions – another reform pressed on and achieved by the 1974 Labour government – went some way to solving this, but an increasing number of union officials were coming to believe that they would need much more of an 'insider's' view in order to pursue issues satisfactorily. Further, unions had, in vastly augmenting their strength since the late 1960s, quite quickly reached the limits of that strength. They could achieve pay increases which led to political controversy and were eroded by inflation; at shop-floor level certain minor improvements in work methods could be secured, but usually by unofficial rather than union action; and the powerful job controls maintained by some of the older crafts were being threatened by new technologies. A breakthrough could only be made by tackling managerial power at the point where it really operated – in the boardroom. According to this view, industrial democracy would provide scope for the extension of collective bargaining.

There was never complete consensus on this. The AUEW, for example, stood firmly by a policy of confrontational bargaining. The GMWU and the electricians' union also feared the blurring of management and union. However, members of the Bullock Committee sympathetic to union interests argued for a national system of industrial democracy. They were joined by those, including Bullock himself, who believed in conciliation, ending the confrontational approach to industrial relations in favour of the pursuit of shared ends. This interpretation was the corollary of the overall changes being attempted by the government at national level in order to establish a more formal and institutional consensus. Worker participation at the industrial level could be seen as a parallel to the involvement of unions in tripartite economic policy discussions.

The Bullock majority made two main proposals. First, in any firm where employees and unions wanted it, employees should have a right to be represented by worker-directors on a single-tier board; the employee-directors would be elected by all *union members* employed in the firm; the number of worker-directors would equal the number of shareholder-directors, with a small group of independents appointed jointly by the two sides making up the complement of the board – what came to be known as the '$2x+y$' formula. Second, the law should be amended to require that the directors of *all* companies should take equal account of the interests of employees and shareholders.

Employer representatives on the Committee dissented and produced their own minority report. They accepted the second proposal, and conceded the principle of board-level representation, but not the basis on which it was proposed to establish it. The industrialists wanted there to be several years' experience with sub-board participation before employee-directors; they rejected the idea of a union base for elections; they wanted subsidiaries of holding companies, financial institutions and subsidiaries of foreign companies excluded: they amended the $2x+y$ formula to ensure that management representatives were included among the *employees'* directors and to increase the number of independents; and they wanted worker representation limited to a top-level supervisory board, with a new management board instituted below this to carry on day-to-day running of the firm, free of employees.

The gap between the majority and the minority could not be bridged; but even then the minority report went far further than most employers in Britain were prepared to go. The CBI reacted with considerable hostility to the report. It refused even to discuss the more radical ideas; it made dire warnings of industrial collapse if the majority report were implemented; and it threatened a general withdrawal of co-operation with the government. The Confederation went to lengths of public propaganda over this issue that it had never tried before, and besides the powerful effect that this had on the matter in hand, the campaign won the CBI new prestige within industry and new member firms.

Several Ministers, including, most prominently, Edmund Dell, Secretary for Trade and the Minister who would have to introduce any relevant legislation, shared many of the CBI's views, and pressed within the government for the dilution of any legislation originating in Bullock. On the other hand, the TUC was exerting little pressure to counter that of the CBI. It remained broadly committed to the Bullock majority position, and lobbied Ministers accordingly; but it was too divided internally to mobilize union action. There had always been opposition to participation among British unions, as has already been noted. Now that the question was for the first time becoming a practical possibility, this opposition became more active. As a recent study by John Elliott summarizes the position:[9]

> The problem was that, in the private sector at least, most union leaders fell into one of three camps – they were either, like the Communists, ideologically opposed to the notion on political grounds; or, like the Electricians, opposed in principle on industrial blurring-the-lines-of-conflict grounds; or, like most of the rest, were unwilling to face up to the challenges involved and instinctively preferred to stick to old-style clear-cut bargaining relationships, especially at a time when economic problems made many boardroom decisions unpalatable to workers.

The cabinet set up its own committee under Shirley Williams, Secretary of State for Education and Paymaster General, to work out an approach acceptable to all involved. Not surprisingly, the White Paper[10] that eventually emerged marked a considerable weakening of the original Bullock proposals. It proposed no universal statutory system, but a gradual approach leaving much to voluntary initiatives by individual unions and managements. Fall-back legislation to which unions seeking participation could have recourse in the event of employer intransigence was proposed on the following lines: in any company employing over 500 workers a Joint Representation Committee of all recognized unions in the firm could require the company board to discuss company strategy with it. After three or four years of this procedure the JRCs in companies of over 2000 employees could call for a ballot of the whole work-force on whether there should be a full scheme of worker participation. If the ballot result were favourable the JRC could claim just one third of the representatives on the top policy-making board of a new two-tier company structure. (The second level, the management board, would exclude worker representatives, and would be responsible for the day-to-day conduct of the enterprise.)

This central proposal, for an essentially German system of representation (though with a lower level of employee representation than now exists in Germany), followed reasonably closely the 'managerial' minority report of Bullock and bore little relation to the majority report. Further, the White Paper was indecisive on several key issues, proposing merely further consultations on such matters as application of the confidentiality rule; whether certain companies (such as banks and multi-nationals) should be excluded from the provisions; and the debate over whether the unions should be the sole channel for the election of employee board representatives.

On the other hand, the issue of participation is unlikely to die. Several unions *and managements* have taken initiatives of their own in the past three years in their search for more constructive solutions to industrial relations problems In 1975 both British Leyland and Chrysler – two automotive firms with a complex history of industrial relations problems – established participative machinery based on shop stewards though falling short of actual decision-making powers. Unions in local government tried to negotiate the participation of employee representatives in local council committees, and the NUM made radical demands for worker control of individual pits. Developments have been particularly rapid in the nationalized industries, and in the *Industrial Democracy* White Paper the government committed itself to particular progress here. So far there have been discussions on participative machinery in most of the energy industries, and the Secretary of State for Energy, Tony Benn, established a national Energy Commission, including workers' representatives, to work out national policy in this important area. The newly nationalized shipbuilding and aerospace industries have a statutory liability to develop industrial democracy, while the most advanced experiment so far has been in the Post Office, where the unions have had a rare long-standing interest in participation. For a trial period of two years the Post Office will be governed very much on Bullock majority lines, by a single-tier board constructed on the $2x+y$ formula; apart from the chairman there will be seven managerial and seven employee representatives and five 'independents' (including two representatives of consumer interests). Equally important, there will also be worker participation at lower decision-making levels.

The second issue which illustrates some of the many continuing areas of stalemate in British industrial relations was the dispute at the Grunwick film processing laboratories in Willsden, West London.[11] This began in summer 1976 when a large group of Asian employees walked out of the factory over some ostensibly minor quarrels with the management, rioted and were summarily dismissed. They joined a trade union, the Association of Professional, Executive, Clerical and Computer Staffs (APEX), and sought reinstatement and union representation. The particular pattern of action that they followed left them vulnerable to certain loopholes in the apparently tight web of workers' rights embodied in the Trade Union and Labour Relations Acts and the Employment Protection Act. Their employer exploited these loopholes with ingenuity and resilience, aided by lawyers from the National Association for Freedom, a newly formed group on the extreme right wing of the Conservative Party.

The workers remained dismissed and the union powerless to represent them. It seemed an extraordinary development in the light of the preceding years' advances in union power. Various sections of the labour movement responded in their own ways but with equally little effect. Certain militant groups organized mass picketing of the kind that had developed in the early 1970s. Large numbers of pickets surrounded the works early in the mornings to try to prevent the non-striking workers from entering. But the firm hired buses to drive through the picket lines, and the Metropolitan Police appeared in large numbers to ensure that they could do so. The main result of these actions was to bring to the television screens pictures of strikers fighting the police, bringing discredit on the entire trade-union movement.

APEX itself and the TUC tried their usual policies of appealing to the idea of 'good industrial relations' and of stigmatizing the firm as a 'rogue employer' that should be brought into line with the new national consensus around the social contract.

The Secretary of State for Employment, Albert Booth, tried familiar techniques of conciliation, but the employer, George Ward, refused to play the traditional game. ACAS tried to carry out a referendum on union membership among the Grunwick work-force, but Mr Ward refused to provide the names and addresses of workers. ACAS then took a referendum among the strikers only. This matter became the subject of protracted legal action, from which the employer emerged victorious. The government also appointed a committee of inquiry under Lord Justice Scarman to investigate the whole issue. True to the traditions of such inquiries it proposed a conciliatory approach, including reinstatement of the dismissed employees and union recognition. But again the firm refused to budge.

The conflict continued intermittently through 1977, and then early in 1978 dribbled to an end as the courts finally ruled in favour of Grunwick in the rather technical dispute with ACAS, and the pickets abandoned their hopeless task which had by then become little more than a symbol.

The dispute was significant in that it drew attention to the position of small employers, who feel excluded from the important new institutions of negotiation and consultation among government, large employers and the representatives of labour (this will be discussed further in Chapter 6). As a result, an entire alternative approach to industrial relations is growing up around this so often neglected sector of capital. It is based on avoiding all close relations between governments and major interests, including a withdrawal from the traditional English approach of compromise and consensus. Contrary to much public opinion, unions do not depend for their strength purely on the threat of industrial action, which is not so easy to wield as might appear. They rely heavily on agreed conventions of behaviour – the *dicta* of committees and courts of inquiry, nudgings and promptings from government departments, tacit norms of conduct. The Grunwick case showed that an employer prepared to 'hard-nose' his way through this web of institutions, allowing no conventions to stand between his freedom and the strict letter of the law, will be able to depend on the police force to assist him in the war of attrition consequent on such a course and can gain important victories. This seemed increasingly to be the main alternative to attempts at rebuilding a tripartite consensus, and one to which the Conservative Party appeared to be more and more attracted. That it should have been prepared to contemplate such a departure from the dominant traditions of British politics is perhaps one of the most impressive indicators of how far that politics had changed by the late 1970s.

PART TWO

Institutions and Groups

Chapter 5

The State

The discussion in Part One deliberately avoided elaborate concepts and theory. To proceed any further this will no longer be possible, though the conceptual apparatus used here will be kept to a minimum. The point is that one cannot read an account of industrial relation in Britain without sensing that some major processes of change have been at work. Any particular example of incomes policy, legislative change or tripartite talks was no doubt undertaken by those involved as just one particular event, a reaction to pressing, often urgent, affairs of the day. But taken together, this mass of individual events adds up to something more coherent, if not consistent. This is not because there has been any secret conspiracy at work, but simply because all the people involved, at any rate within government and employers' organizations, have been trying to pursue a roughly similar objective under a persistent set of pressures and constraints. The objective has been to maintain and enhance the stability and productivity of the British economy. The constraints have included a continuing dependence for economic progress on a primarily privately owned economy under circumstances of full employment and a strong, decentralized trade-union movement – circumstances which upset the historical balance of such an economy without erecting any lasting balancing mechanisms in its place. For a period it did seem that something had been erected: as was noted in Chapters 1 and 2, economic growth and rising mass prosperity provided a source of stability for several years. In many ways the intensification of the search for new policies can be measured alongside the declining capacity of the growth mechanism.

Such a pattern of constraints provides only limited

scope for variation in the strategies which different groups adopt. In trying to grasp the changes involved, use will here be made of just two concepts: liberalism and corporatism. By themselves they are not really adequate to the task, and within the scope of the present work it will not be possible even to give a full account of them. I have developed this whole question in more detail in my *Class Conflict and the Industrial Relations Crisis,*[1] and those interested in pursuing the subject further are referred to that.

Liberalism and its associated adjectives are nowadays used very loosely indeed, often referring to little more than actions which are easygoing, unconstrained or vaguely progressive. Historically it refers to something much stronger and rather different:[2] to the process whereby – in the emergence of the modern world out of feudalism – the political, economic and moral spheres of life became freed from entanglement with one another and the individual became liberated from the traditional obligations which had bound him to groups and loyalties. But this freedom did not mean licence or anarchy. To take the most important case and the one most central to our concerns, behaviour *within* the economy was strictly controlled by the market. Freedom from interference by the state in the economy meant allowing market forces to work without interference. Similarly, individualism meant liberty for the individual to grasp opportunities available to him; but it also meant being forced to remain as an individual and not combine with others.

The implications of this for the position of labour are as follows: in theory, wages would reach their most efficient level if individual capitalists bargained with individual workers for the price of the latter's labour. Provided no one interfered with this process, a price would be reached which represented the best deal each side could achieve in the prevailing conditions of supply and demand. But three amendments must immediately be made to the model if it is to bear any relation to reality.

First, although we speak of the individual capitalist, we really mean the individual firm, for the firm is the unit that employs labour. Only in the case of the truly one-man firm is capital represented by an individual human; in all other cases the employing unit is an organization – an organization which was and is regarded in law as an 'individual'. The worker is, however, a real individual; workers are not usually hired as organized groups, but singly. Second, although the contract between master and man is in principle a free exchange between two equal partners, once the worker has been hired he puts himself under the control of the employer; the relationship ceases to be one of exchange and becomes one of authority. Finally, there is a major contrast in the position of labour and capital which reduces considerably the implications of equality in the phrase 'free exchange'. If the worker does not work he has no means of supporting himself (or his family); he has to work to survive, and in his search for acceptable work he is limited by the very real physical constraints of personal movement. Capital, in the form of money, can, on the other hand, be moved at will so long as there are efficient money markets. Even capital in the form of factories and machines can be sold and bought relatively easily, so that the capitalist can find the most profitable place for his investment. And if the worst comes to the worst the capitalist can temporarily live off his capital. It is these differences which make possible the central feature of labour relations under capitalism: the subordination of working men to the authority of the organization which employs them.

Not surprisingly, from early on workers began to try to improve the terms of this subordination by organizing themselves. If, instead of facing capital as individuals they combined together, refusing both to work themselves and (if possible) preventing anyone else from working unless the terms of their employment were improved, they could offset some of the inequalities from which they suffered in the labour contract, though probably at the expense of some reduction in the number of them who would be employed. But combination of that kind broke liberalism's rule of individualism.

Liberalism, that is economic liberalism, was therefore a system of social control, of very tight control. Such a system never really existed in its pure form; the state, for example, was rarely absent from some kind of economic intervention. But compared with what went before and what went after, the period of economic liberalism (in England from the late eighteenth to the late nineteenth centuries) was notable for the autonomy of the economic process and for individualism.[3] One crucial development within it was the gradual acceptance of trade unions, of collectivism. This weakened the importance of the subordination of labour through individualism, and at certain moments in history was a source of considerable political controversy and fears of social upheaval. But unionism grew very slowly in Britain. The nineteenth-century economy, backed by the vast resources of the empire, was strong; in general the unions could be accommodated to the rules of the British political system. Gradually, liberalism accommodated itself to collectivism.

The possibility of a collective liberalism opened the possibility of a liberal economy in which labour, far from being rigorously subordinated, would be strong and able to win unprecedented political and economic concessions. It is not possible here to trace all the developments in this process.[4] However, by the Second World War the spread of unionism and the new official commitment to maintaining full employment marked a major strengthening of the position of labour within a pattern of liberal collectivism. Given the importance of individualism in subordinating labour with classical liberal capitalism, how was such a rise in labour's position possible without a major challenge to the system of economic organization? The answer was given in Chapter 1 when the basis of the post-war consensus was set out: full employment; the involvement of unions in policy-making; the depoliticization of industrial relations; consensus over the construction of the welfare state; and a centralized trade-union leadership capable of restraining its members. As these declined in importance, so economic prosperity provided a new basis of order, enabling workers' demands to be satisfied within the terms of the existing economic order – accompanied occasionally by increases in unemployment to check labour's power at moments of economic difficulty.

Thus a predominantly liberal pattern of industrial relations persisted on amended terms. The two sides of industry remained separate from each other, jealously guarding their autonomy and accepting a degree of conflict in their relationship (replacing the separation of individuals in the classical formation); the government abstained from detailed involvement in industrial issues – the tradition of voluntarism; and as explained in Chapter 1, the law remained individualistically liberal, occasionally creating difficulties for the unions but also enabling them to emerge and define themselves autonomously and without state interference. One achievement of capitalist liberalism had been to free the economic market from interference from 'moral' factors, such as the medieval doctrine of the just wage. This also remained; the mediation and arbitration services developed by the Ministry of Labour did not try to rule on what a particular wage 'ought' to be, but tried to reach the solution which the bargaining partners would have reached had they been able to secure agreement – a kind of analogy to the market process.

However, those features of the post-war consensus listed above are not strictly compatible with a liberal model. To understand them it is useful to consider the second concept to be introduced here: corporatism.

The idea of corporatism, or the corporate state, which has its origins in nineteenth-century Roman Catholic social thought, refers to a system of politico-economic organization that is fundamentally different from liberalism.[5] The economy remains capitalist in the sense of being privately owned, but the stability of the system is ensured through the close *integration* of political, economic and moral forces, rather than through their separation. And workers (and others) are subordinated, not through individualism, but through the very fact of belonging to collectivities, organizations; the organizations which represent them also regulate them.

As a fully fledged system of social organization, corporatism is encountered even less frequently than full liberalism. But, like liberalism, it is often a useful model to apply when trying to bring out certain characteristics of a society in contrast to others. As soon as a capitalist society develops trade unions, large units of capital and detailed state intervention in the economy, there is a departure from the rules of liberalism; and the deficiency is likely to be met by some development of the rules of corporatism. It is possible to regard the continuing strong liberalism in Britain's post-war industrial relations system as paradoxically being made possible by certain elements of corporatism (alongside the reliance on prosperity). The involvement of the unions in policy-making, and consensus over post-war reconstruction, the welfare state and the removal of industrial relations from political conflict provided a moral unity among government, employers and union leaders, leading these last to be willing to use their organizational centralization and strength to restrain rather than press the demands of their members.

As first this and then growth declined, the potential instability of a collective liberalism under full employment became increasingly problematic. Most of the responses of government to this situation can be seen as attempts at introducing new elements of corporatism, albeit not consciously. The fact that they were doing so under conditions of emergency, without the legacy of implicit agreements and understandings which war had bequeathed in the 1940s, and with a trade-union movement the power of which was no longer concentrated in the leadership, meant that the policies adopted became more obviously corporatist, as will be discussed below.

In all of this the state is a crucial institution; it is the only actor in the situation which can change the rules of the system. The unions are primarily defensive organizations, while employers are fragmented and competing with one another. Even an organization like the CBI could not by itself engineer a change in the conduct of industrial relations, because it has had no power to force individual firms, or even individual industry-level associations, to toe a common line. No matter how far employers might agree in principle on the approach to unions which would be in their best interest, in the practical case an individual firm will pursue the path that brings it most rewards and fewer costs, for that is the only way it stays in business; and if that means ignoring an agreed line among employers, then so be it. This is not equally true of some other societies. For example, in Japan the small group of giant firms which dominates the economy is so closely related to the ruling Liberal Democratic Party that it is difficult to distinguish the initiatives of government from those of industry.[6] In Italy the state is so weak and governments so unstable that several initiatives in policy have come from a group of large employers approaching the unions. In West Germany, Sweden and the Netherlands employers' associations have a degree of power over their members which enables them to co-ordinate policy among employers, disciplining member firms.[7] In Britain, however, the power of associations has been weak, and so far the recent increase in the concentration of industrial holdings has not affected this. This leaves the state with a particularly heavy liability for policy innovation.

While the 'state' is often used loosely as a synonym for 'government', there is strictly a distinction, the former being a more encompassing term including such institutions as the monarchy, the armed forces, the police, the law and judiciary as well as the more familiar organs of government – which itself comprises both a political and an administrative (civil service) element. Attention here will concentrate on government, as the most active element in the state for our purposes, including separate consideration of the positions of the two major parties which have formed governments during the period under review. However, there will also be some discussion of the role of the judiciary and the police, which have to a certain extent played an independent part.

The role of government

Modern governments juggle four not easily compatible goals of economic policy: full employment, price stability, a favourable balance of payments and protection of the exchange rate of the currency. If any of these is neglected there is a risk of major instability. The main problem is the relationship between full employment and price stability. Policies which maintain the former are likely to result in price inflation. This in turn is likely to worsen the country's balance of payments, reducing confidence in the government's ability to hold the rate of exchange, a fact which is in itself likely to cause an exchange crisis. Since the war British governments have been quite reluctant to raise unemployment in order to avoid the problem of inflation, as was shown in Part One. They have therefore used various devices to make it less likely that a high level of employment will result in wage increases which will in turn push up prices – in other words, policies that will prevent workers from taking advantage, whether through union action or simply through the operation of the market, of the opportunities which full employment affords them. Incomes policy is, of course, the prime example of this and, as Part One showed, there have been several waves of incomes policy in Britain over the past two decades, though no one example has survived for more than a few years.

Incomes policy has important corporatist implications: there is an attempt at tripartite agreement on the criteria for acceptable pay increases (including criteria of entitlement to pay which are not necessarily those of the market); an attempt at securing the agreement of unions to ensure that their members keep to the restraint policy; and the government uses a political authority to regulate an economic process. Some of the reasons for governments ceasing to support incomes policies are specific to the political parties and will be considered under that head, but others have to do with more general problems. An incomes policy distorts differentials, market forces and the agreed assumptions of bargaining partners. As time passes it therefore becomes increasingly difficult to hold the line, with workers, unions and employers all finding themselves constrained. The policy thus becomes an object of political controversy: there are breaches of its rules, and the government has to decide whether to allow the policy to become increasingly ragged or to take stronger coercive powers to maintain it, courting further conflict. There are therefore good reasons for expecting incomes policy to continue to be used – it is crucial to affecting the unemployment/inflation trade-off, especially when many unionized workers might not be affected by unemployment – but also for there to be recurrent disillusion with the policies.[8]

As was discussed in Chapter 3, both Labour and Conservative governments in the 1968-72 period turned to industrial relations law reform as an alternative to incomes policy; it was believed that this would not be so vulnerable to political controversy as incomes policy. The law could affect the level of wage increases in several ways. By making strikes more difficult it would make it harder for workers to press wage claims. By making unions liable for ensuring that their members kept to agreements – a highly corporatist provision – it would reduce unofficial pressure for increases. Reducing strikes might also improve the efficiency of the economy, and (in the Conservative version) measures for making the closed shop difficult to achieve might weaken unions' power by reducing their membership – this last being incidentally a highly anti-corporatist, neo-liberal policy in that it weakens the role of organization.

If successful, such policies would remove from governments the onus of constant detailed and unpopular interventions. British politicians looked wistfully at West Germany, the USA, Sweden and certain other countries where legal provisions designed to make strikes difficult were already established. This was partly misleading, because in major waves of primarily unofficial action, such as Britain and several other countries were facing in the late 1960s and early 1970s, such laws often proved impossible to use. Even more important, while having these laws already on the statute book might keep the issue out of politics, the act of introducing them is itself, of course, a highly political operation, and British governments were doing this at a time of considerable labour strength. As the Conservative experience showed, the very existence of the Industrial Relations Act actually increased the number of strikes; it also soured relations between government and unions at a time when the government badly needed tripartite understanding; while the reluctance of employers to risk intensified conflict made them unwilling to take advantage of its provisions – there were virtually no gains to compensate for the losses.

There will probably be future attempts by governments at legal intervention to reduce the power of organized labour, though probably not on the ambitious scale of the 1971 Act. Governments unable or unwilling for various reasons to use incomes policy or reach mutual understandings with the unions may well fall back on some kind of legal restraints. They will be encouraged in this by the fact that public-opinion polls regularly report the unpopularity of certain trade-union practices, such as the closed shop; and governments are often liable to exaggerate the significance in terms of real political force of opinion polls.

The attempt at involving union leaders and major employers in tripartite relationships is a less risky strategy for governments. The object is to secure a commitment to restraint in exchange for a share in economic policy – though the latter may well mean little more than presenting the unions with the government's view of likely developments in the economy and hoping to persuade them to accept that view and the priorities which flow from it. Understandings of this kind were important in the war years and immediately afterwards, but, as was pointed out in Chapter 1, the very special priorities of that period could not have been permanent. Attempts at reconstructing something similar have not been very successful unless they remain at the level of uncontroversial or long-term policy – in which case they are not very effective in tempting the unions into a commitment to restraint. These policies cost little but gain little. To move further means involving the unions in a more tangible share in decisions, which may actually mean conceding power, and this is no longer safe, uncontroversial politics. A prime example were the talks between Edward Heath and the unions in 1972. The Prime Minister said he would take the CBI and the TUC into policy-making across the whole range of government decisions, in exchange for which he expected a commitment to wage and price restraint. The unions took him at his word and made policy demands across a wide front. The Ministers decided that this was an attempt to interfere in the government's prerogative to make policy, and the talks failed to result in agreement.

The 1974 Labour government was able to reach such an agreement with the unions; it gave them a much greater role in policy-making, and in exchange they delivered a remarkable degree of restraint, though on closer examination neither side of the exchange was quite as dramatic as might at first seem to be the case. The policies conceded to the unions were largely those which increased their own organizational strength: the two Trade Union and Labour Relations Acts and the Employment Protection Act; representation on a range of tripartite decision-making bodies; the repeal of the Industrial Relations Act; favourable government intervention following continuing clashes between the unions and the courts. They had far less success in affecting overall economic policy, apart perhaps from achieving certain taxation changes in the government's first years. On the level of unemployment, public spending cuts, import controls, government intervention through planning agreements, the TUC gained virtually nothing after 1975. It was, however, during this very period that the unions conceded most in terms of wage restraint; though the amendment necessary on this side of the balance is that the high level of unemployment had anyway weakened labour's power to make demands.

With occasional exceptions in Conservative policy, the move towards increasing use of tripartite devices is the most consistent and persistent tendency in policy over the past fifteen years or so. It constitutes an interesting and potentially very significant shift in the stance of governments on the politics of industrial relations, as can be seen from the changes which took place in the position of the Ministry of Labour. In the post-war years the Ministry was the symbol of bi-partisan consensus; a department standing apart from the rest of government policy in order to pursue conciliation. As the pace of government intervention quickened with the growing economic problem, so this role was compromised and the department became increasingly the instrument of an incomes policy directed at ensuring wage restraint. The apogee of this period was reached in the years 1968 to 1973 when the Ministry, now the Department of Employment (and Productivity) was first, under Labour, the department administering incomes policy and next, under the Tories, the guardian of the Industrial Relations Act. Since then the functions of the DE have been virtually dismembered, and in every case have been delegated to a tripartite body: the conciliation services to ACAS; the management of employment exchanges and policy on manpower and employment to the

Manpower Services Commission; health, safety and factory inspection to the Health and Safety Commission; even incomes policy itself to understandings between the Treasury, the TUC and the CBI.

In many eyes, tripartitism represents the essence of corporatism. There is obviously much truth in this, though one's assessment of its significance must depend on exactly what is going on in the tripartite exchange. In full corporatism union leaders accept the priorities determined by government and employers and then impose the required restraint on their members. If instead the leaders press for major concessions from governments in exchange for the restraint they will offer, then much of this rigidly hierarchical, anti-pluralistic implication of corporatism is lost. This is a theme to which we shall return in Part Three.

Finally, it is necessary to consider a strategy of a very different kind which is becoming increasingly important: the return to high unemployment, maintained in particular by government acceptance of the need to keep tight control over the growth of the money supply. This policy, which has recently been adopted by most Western governments, constitutes a significant *volte-face* on the whole tendency of post-war full-employment policy. As such it is a return to the means of economic regulation characteristic of classical liberalism, and thus the opposite of corporatism. It is an indication of the depth of the current economic crisis that it appears in most countries (including Britain) not as an alternative to corporatist policies, but alongside, supplementing them. This is a paradox to which we shall return in Part Three.

The positions of the parties[9]

So far 'government' has been treated as a more or less undifferentiated category, but the government has been in the hands of the Labour and Conservative Parties at different points during this period. What have these differences contributed to industrial relations policy? The party base of government is certainly among the factors affecting policy, though it would be a mistake to regard it as of over-riding significance. For example, the change of government in 1951 really only accelerated trends away from economic controls and close government/union relations which had already begun under Labour. The change towards both planning and incomes policy in 1961 occurred without a change of government, though it took the return of Labour to produce a fuller (but temporary) commitment to these. By 1968 this line of policy had run into the ground and the switch to attempts at reforming trade-union law occurred while Labour was still in office. On the other hand, the major attempt at law reform was a distinctive Conservative policy, as was the deliberate reduction of government/union contacts which also dated from 1970. In 1972, however, what has been possibly the most dramatic shift in industrial relations policy since the war (towards tight incomes policy, considerable general economic intervention and detailed tripartite contact) was carried out by the Conservatives while still in office. The change of government in February 1974, during and as a result of an industrial relations crisis, would seem to constitute a clear case of the importance of party difference. While recognizing this, it is important to note the important elements of continuity: intensive tripartitism has survived, and it is possible to regard the temporary interruption of incomes policy in 1974-5 as virtually inevitable whatever party was in power given the strength of the inflationary shock administered by the Arab oil cartel. On the other hand Labour's ability to capitalize on trade-union support has been a particularly distinctive feature of these past few years.

As is so often the case, the parties' policies seem most distinctive when they are in opposition or in the first few months of government. An administration settled in office becomes prey to the great constraints of the country's economic position and the lobbying of pressure groups which between them erode partisan distinctiveness. The following appear to be the main attributes of the party differences that do express themselves – differences which have become much sharper as the crisis has deepened, at least in the stance of parties if not in the policies of governments.

Conservatives tend to hanker after the abolition of organized structures of government planning and a return to free-market policies. The solution to industrial relations problems is seen as automatically taken care of by the level of unemployment, perhaps backed by legislation that will make strike action more difficult. Industrial relations are then depoliticized; trade unions settle down to a non-political role of industrial bargaining; and the government can revert to a role of occasional conciliation in difficult disputes, not having to bother with incomes policy or troublesome tripartite deals that smack of corporatism and concede too much power to the unions. In opposition and in early months of government Conservatives are likely to move in this direction, and their right, *laissez faire* wing is likely to want strong versions of these policies at all times. But Conservative governments have not pursued this line for long periods or in more than superficial ways. As we have seen, far from depoliticizing industrial relations, such policies intensify the level of conflict; governments find themselves intervening in the economy anyway, for reasons that have little to do with trade unions; and the level of unemployment which is necessary if reliance is placed on this mechanism alone to restrain wages, may be very high indeed. Recently these 'tough-minded' Conservative policies have been supplemented by certain additional weapons which might avoid the need for compromises with union leaders: attempts at stirring up public hostility against strikers, and greater reliance on the police and possibly the armed forces to break strikes.

The alternative strategy, favoured by 'moderate' Conservatives and towards which Conservative governments tend to gravitate, involves some use of free-market policies, but supplemented by corporatist measures for incorporating the unions; tripartite measures, informal understandings and incomes policies are used in order to construct a dialogue with union leaders and seek their agreement to restraint in order to avoid high unemployment as the alternative.

The Labour Party's left wing usually has even less chance to get near policy-making than the Conservative right, and its strategy for industrial relations is not particularly clear. In the 1950s the old Bevanite left had little time for trade unions, whose predominantly right-wing leaders were the left's opponents within the party. The left's policies for state ownership and planning therefore gave little consideration to the problems these would pose for autonomous unions. This began to change by the early 1960s as the political stance of several major unions shifted to the left, and during the 1966 Labour government it was the Labour left, the Tribune Group, which provided the core of opposition to incomes policy and industrial relations legislation. The left is now wedded firmly to support for free collective bargaining, though this combines uneasily with its advocacy of government planning elsewhere in the economy. It is then argued that voluntary restraint would be possible in a planned, non-capitalist economy based on social justice.

A more recent and more sophisticated version of the traditional left-wing strategy is that associated with Tony Benn, and relates policies for socialist planning more closely to the pursuit of industrial efficiency and high investment. Central to this is a commitment to powerful worker participation in management through union channels. These policies would seem to imply income restraint, though it is not yet clear where all advocates of this strategy stand on the issue of incomes policy. The strategy has not yet had any chance of being implemented, although for a period in 1974-5 it seemed that it might be a central part of the government's strategy.

The Labour right has been more effectively in command of the party's policies in office – though, as with the Conservative moderates, it is difficult to distinguish preferred policies as such from those which, as a government, it feels bound to pursue given the pressures which exist. Apart from the 1966-70 period, when it came to treat them as little more than a nuisance, the Labour right has placed considerable weight on close understandings with trade-union leaders; it is distinctly averse to shop-floor militancy. It seeks economic stability by building on these understandings, alongside a moderate level of state intervention in the economy in order to pursue economic growth. Its position thus approximates fairly closely to that of the Tory left, though as a Labour Party it is able and willing to place more stress on links with the unions and less on market forces.

It is therefore the two 'moderate' wings of the major parties, with their essentially similar approaches, which tend to dominate policy, and which are most clearly associated with the policies which have been called corporatist.

The judiciary and the police

The role of the judiciary in industrial relations has been extensively treated by John Griffith in another volume in this series, *The Politics of the Judiciary*.[10] He there argues the general case that judges, for reasons of background and training, tend to adopt conservative (even Conservative) positions in several areas where they have discretion – industrial relations being one of them. And of the Industrial Relations Act in particular he suggests that 'the identification of "law" and "policy" made almost impossible the continuance of the interplay between the judges and politicians which had provided a valuable tolerance' and goes on to marvel at the judiciary's willingness to lend themselves to the political manoeuvring embodied in the Act.

Like several other observers, Griffith attributes the apparent bias of judges in their treatment of trade-union issues largely to their position as members of the upper middle class, subject to the prejudices of public opinion within that class. There may well be important elements of truth in this. Several of the important moments at which the courts have redefined union immunities in order to prevent some form of union action have co-incided with shifts in general opinion against unions. It may, however, be at least equally useful to emphasize a different aspect, discussed in Chapter 1. English Common Law has remained firmly based in the individualist liberal tradition, under which nearly all the actions of combinations like trade unions are virtually certain to be illegal; and nineteenth- and early twentieth-century legislators, anxious not to disturb this basic liberal mould, gave unions their legal right to existence by granting immunities from what would otherwise be the sanctions of the law – in contrast with an alternative pursued in some other countries of constructing a positive law to define the place of combinations. This means that in any case where the scope of the legal immunity is unclear, the judiciary, as guardian of the liberal tradition of Common Law, is likely to revert to a logic of reasoning hostile to combinations.

The recent spate of legislation provides a more extensive structure of positive trade-union law than has existed in the past, but it does not change fundamentally the liberal base. The concept of the Common Law immunity, now considerably enlarged in its scope, remains at the heart of things. Unions prefer matters this way; the alternative would be law which prescribed under what conditions industrial action was legal and who had the right to take it, which would almost certainly be more restrictive than the present situation. It is, however, likely that conflicts with the courts will continue in future years.

Until a few years ago, a book on the politics of industrial relations would have had little occasion to mention the police, apart from occasional conflicts between them and pickets. Recently, however, they have come to be major actors in important strikes, often being used to provide sheer mass numbers to confront, sometimes physically, mass numbers of strikers and demonstrators. In the great strikes of the early 1970s – such as the coal disputes of 1972 and 1973-4 and the building strike of 1972 – they were used to combat mass pickets and flying pickets. More recently, in the long-running Grunwick dispute, the police were used to ensure that non-striking workers were able to defy attempts to prevent the works from opening.

In all these cases the police appear unequivocally on the 'side' of the employer in a dispute. Since it is the strikers who are trying to interfere with the normal running of business activity, it is they who are likely to infringe the law by obstruction and similar offences. These incidents have also provided street scenes of open conflict, rare in England, which were featured prominently by the press and television to the detriment of any serious consideration of the issues at stake. The vivid portrayal of strikers fighting the police was used by the opponents of the unions to associate them with disorder, violence and the breakdown of the rule of law. Less dramatic but at least as important has been recent evidence of the activities of the Special Branch gathering information on industrial militants, for purposes which are never adequately disclosed. All these events have brought the police into a controversial area of industrial conflict, which they have traditionally tried to avoid.

This position of the police can be explained in terms of the increasing level of industrial conflict of the past decade. The use, since the early 1970s, of the mass picket by strikers obviously creates a problem of order on the streets and goes beyond the right of peaceful picketing entrenched in law. The mass picket, in turn, has been developed because of the increasing resistance of governments and employers to union claims. During the 1950s and 1960s strikes were usually short, ending in either compromise or mediation of some kind. More recently they have become more clearly wars of attrition, in which each side waits for the other to weaken. In these circumstances strikers (on whose side time never stands, given their need to earn money in order to live) look for weapons to weaken their opponent, such as ensuring that all work on the site in question is totally stopped. Once the technique was developed, it was applied to other situations of employer intransigence, of which Grunwick is the prime example.

One factor which makes the ordinary law of picketing of little use as guidance to either police or strikers is the importance of lorries in bringing supplies to a firm or, in the case of Grunwick, of buses in bringing non-strikers through the factory gates to work. The law on picketing, devised before the days of modern transport, gives strikers the right to try to persuade people to support a strike, provided they use peaceful means. It is not possible for a small number of pickets to stop a lorry or bus by peaceful means; hence the mass picket. The TUC has tried to have the law changed to give pickets the right to stop vehicles. This would of course mean the police virtually assisting strikers in stopping traffic in order to argue with the occupants, and even the Labour government at the height of the social contract balked at this.

Some observers have seen the increasing use of the police in conflicts as an aspect of the rise of the corporate state, on the grounds that corporatism implies strong state intervention. In my view this is fundamentally mistaken. Corporatism does not mean just *any* increase in state power, but the particular phenomenon of the state orchestrating hierarchically arranged organized groups. Further, the classic liberal political economy only excluded state intervention in the sense of interference with market processes; it by no means excluded strong police action.

If a market economy is working 'properly', there is little

need for an active police role in controlling labour; if a corporatist economy is working 'properly', the integration of organizations similarly renders a police role unimportant. In either case, if the police are active it means that the normal system of social and economic regulation is breaking down. That the forces of law and order have become more openly involved at the same time that *both* corporatist policies *and* the opposite development of reliance of high unemployment have been adopted is evidence of the growing difficulties of government in maintaining any kind of stability in industrial relations and of the depth of the prevailing crisis.

Chapter 6

Capital

To speak of capital rather than industry or employers is to adopt the classic economic division between capital and labour as factors of production. Abstractions though these may be, they do have a very tangible meaning in the tripartite structures which are so prominent in modern industrial relations politics. Industrial relations are concerned with the terms in which labour is employed, and this is automatically a question of relations between capital and labour. It is in the general interest of labour to increase its price, to reduce its work burden and to gain control over its own development. Capital's interests are the opposite: to reduce the price of labour, to increase the amount of work that can be extracted and to subordinate labour to managerial control.

For some purposes, such an analysis is not affected by whether capital is owned by private persons or the state — so long as it is separate from the work-force. Examples of situations where there is no systematic division between capital and labour are workers' co-operatives and self-managed enterprises on the Yugoslavian model. Under private ownership, capital's interests are ultimately those of private individuals, who seek to maximize the return on their fortune. When the state employs labour, the criterion is still to a large extent the pursuit of a certain rate of return because the government, especially elected politicians, desperately need economic success; however, there is some scope for governments to pursue other, non-economic goals. Within an economy like the British, with the majority of industry in private ownership, the similarity between the behaviour of private and public capital goes further. Public employment takes many cues from the private sector on such matters as pay and investment, and must of course make its way within a market system. Things might be different in various ways in an entirely or predominantly state-owned economy; it is, for example, doubtful whether free trade unions could survive. Overall, therefore, there is little difficulty in including public employment under the heading of capital; and there are indeed only a few systematic differences in industrial relations practice between the two sectors.

On the other hand, 'capital' is not a simple entity, and it will be discussed here in sections.[1] First, attention will be concentrated on large-scale and medium-scale domestic industrial firms in predominantly private ownership – the large British corporations for whom the CBI primarily speaks, whose firms are usually unionized and whom we normally think of as 'the employers'. Most of the statements under this heading will also apply to multi-national firms and to the public sector. However, certain specific features of both these make necessary separate supplementary discussions of them. Attention will then be given to small capital, which increasingly seems to be left out of the system of tripartite relations, and finally to finance capital which includes analysis of capital as an international force.

Industrial capital

British employers have for many years been organized in employers' associations.[2] Originally these were little more than means for combating trade-union demands, but over the years they have acquired certain technical functions and have been the central institutions on the employers' side in the established machinery of collective bargaining. Since the mid-1950s this role has been supplemented (in several cases displaced) by the growth of plant-level bargaining. Since the late 1960s this has been joined by bargaining at the company level – reflecting the increasing size of companies, the preference of multi-national (especially foreign owned) corporations to bargain outside the framework of employers' associations, and an attempt by management at countering shop-floor initiatives. The membership of an association corresponds roughly to the contours of an industry, though this is itself no simple definition, and sometimes the local districts which form the units of the associations have an independent importance in local negotiating – such as the Coventry and District Engineering Employers Association, itself a member of the Engineering Employers Federation.

Nationally, these associations used to be organized under the loose umbrella of the British Employers Confederation. This was separate from the Federation of British Industry, made up of trade associations, which represented firms' industrial as opposed to industrial relations interests.[3] In 1965 these two amalgamated, together with the National Association of British Manufacturers (an organization representing smaller companies), to form the Confederation of British Industry.[4] There has since then been a single powerful representative voice of British industry; its formation was indeed a response to growing state involvement in industrial affairs. The CBI does not only represent manufacturing industry, but other productive sectors as well as commerce and service employment. The nationalized industries are also members; they share in the framing of industrial relations policy but not in policy on the question of public ownership itself (enabling the CBI to maintain its strong hostility to nationalization).

Industry's organizations, and the CBI in particular, often complain that they do not have the same political influence as the TUC – especially, but by no means exclusively, when a Labour government is in office. This is probably true at the level of purely political lobbying and manipulation, but to concentrate on this alone is misleading. Any government seeking economic success but having (or choosing) to do so within the prevailing structure of economic ownership simply must take industry's professed needs into account, because it is on private industry that economic growth largely depends. A good illustration of this point is afforded by the Labour government; after 1975, when the government seemed finally to turn its back on any radical change in relations between the government and private industry, economic policy came increasingly to suit industry's needs, especially as voiced by the CBI – the eventual rejection of the Bullock Report is a case in point. This is not to say that the CBI or industry in general always get what they want; clearly they don't. But any attempt to evaluate their success should not look alone at overt lobbying but at other ways in which industry's demands become paramount.

Nevertheless, it is true that employers have been considerably perplexed by what they have felt to be the excessive power of labour in the post-war economy. They see evidence of this power, not so much in the rate of increase of earnings, as in the fact that this takes place beyond their control; in strikes, especially unexpected unofficial ones; and in the way that in several sectors workers exercise considerable *de facto* control over the conduct of work. But what, in a liberal society with full employment and free trade unions, can be done about it? Most of the time employers come to terms with unions, make compromises, establish *modi vivendi* and build up relations of give and take with shop stewards and local union officials – that is, assuming that they are unable to exclude unions from their firms altogether. Where individual employers are concerned the solution to many problems has been to absorb wage increases by putting up prices. Given the imperfect state of competition in many industries, and the likelihood that unions would ensure that gains in one segment of an industry would be used as precedents to gain similar increases elsewhere, there was little fear of being priced out of the market – at least, not the domestic market. Further, given the government's commitment to full employment, firms could feel reasonably confident that rising prices would not lead to major reductions in demand. At the level of the overall system the consequence of all this was, of course, inflation. But the individual firm, like the individual worker or union, does not operate at the level of the overall system; and besides, so long as the economy was constantly expanding the level of inflation remained low and broadly tolerable. When it threatened to go higher, industry called, often with success, for a temporary increase in unemployment.

But, as Part One showed, over the years this proved less and less adequate and industry, through the CBI, has called for state action of various kinds to strengthen employers' hands against their organized work-force. Its problem here is that, in general, industry does not like government involvement in its affairs. Incomes policy in particular presents problems.[5] It is likely to bring price or profit restraint in its train; it removes from firms their autonomy in setting pay levels and reaching agreements with their own workers; it makes likely repeated interference in a firm's affairs by government agencies; and once the process of intervention starts it may well spread to other issues. The problem is most striking at the level of the individual firm, which may find its particular position in labour or product markets threatened by the application to it of a general policy. At the level of the associations, and particularly of the CBI itself, there is more likely to be some support for incomes policy; if income restraint can be universally secured, labour costs can be held in check, and this must always be to capital's advantage. The CBI and before it the BEC have therefore given general support to incomes policy initiatives, though with considerable reluctance in the late 1960s. The Confederation does however prefer broad, general controls to specific interventions.

Within industry there is therefore declining support for incomes policy the further one moves from the national centre towards the level of the individual firm or plant. At the centre, government, with overall responsibilities for the stability of the economy, turns frequently to incomes policy. Somewhat less enthusiastic, but nevertheless supportive, is the level of industry's own representative bodies. More reluctant, if not downright hostile, are individual firms, who experience the policy not in terms of its potential achievements for the system as a whole but as a more or less arbitrary interference in their business. As we shall see, this feeling is greater still within the small firm.

It was largely in frustration at incomes policy that the CBI and various industry-level federations turned to trade-union law reform in the late 1960s. This seemed to offer fewer problems of government interference. Intractable cases would be dealt with by the law courts, and in general an onus would be placed on unions themselves to keep their members in order. In addition to avoiding government interference, the CBI was anxious to avoid employers themselves becoming involved in controversial litigation with their own employees.[6] The task of possibly taking workers to court they preferred to be left to government – such action would not constitute government intervention in the affairs of the business. As explained in Chapter 3, in the event things turned out rather differently. There was no real agreement between employers and the government, both hoping to slough off on to the other the job of taking unions to court. More generally, whatever support the big associations and the CBI gave, individual firms (or, more likely, individual managers) found the Industrial Relations Act more of a nuisance than a help. Given the extreme hostility of the unions towards it, any attempt by management to invoke, say, its provisions for making agreements legally enforceable would disturb the delicate balance of understandings with local union officers. Also, where the closed shop was concerned, a kind of private corporatism often operated in industry which this libertarian feature of the Act threatened; where unions tried to restrain their members' demands, the threat of expulsion from the union provided a big sanction on militant members since it would automatically involve dismissal from work.[7] (Further, as the EEF disarmingly argued in an ambivalent statement on the closed shop in 1976, where union membership is compulsory unions do not need to keep proving their worth to employees by raising militant demands.)

The CBI loyally defended the Conservatives' Act in public, whatever their members' reservations about actually using it. When the Confederation's Director-General, Campbell Adamson, made an unguarded remark critical of it during the February 1974 election campaign, he was rebuked by several senior businessmen. However, industry has subsequently made no demands for the return of the Act.

The separate question of tripartite talks has been entered by organized employers in various moods. Apart from the immediate post-war years and the period 1961-5, industry has always been hostile towards government planning of any substance. It has, however, been quite happy with the NEDC and, in particular, its associated economic development committees for individual industries. In the technical work of these bodies employers are much better placed in relation to the unions than they are in the task of political lobbying.[8] The unions tend to lack expertise on technical industrial questions that are by nature the province of management. These forums are therefore useful to employers in trying to persuade unions to see their point of view and agree to measures which they might not otherwise support. If the information flow really is unidirectional in this sense, then these bodies are a working example of corporatism. Employers have joined national-level political talks with government and unions with similar intentions, but the more political nature of these exercises makes them more wary. They will try to ensure that the unions do not use these platforms for major policy-making exercises. Certainly the CBI prefers tripartitism to the kind of government-TUC bipartitism that seemed to be developing in the first year of the 1974 Labour government. An indication of the lack of room for manoeuvre available to the CBI as late as 1976 was its passive acceptance of the TUC's terms for a renewed incomes policy – though of course the mere fact that this was a policy of wage restraint marked a major shift towards the employers in the balance of advantage. There was evidence of increased employer commitment to national bodies of this kind in 1977 when the CBI proposed in its discussion document *The Future of Pay Determination* that every year a national forum should be convened to discuss economic strategy before the Budget, comprising representatives from parliament, government, both sides of industry and others. This would be associated with a reform of pay bargaining so that all important negotiations would be concentrated in a short period following the Budget.

In principle the solution that industry most prefers for its industrial relations problems is strict demand management, with increases in the level of unemployment keeping both labour's wage demands and workers' ability to challenge managerial power in general in check. But in the present state of political economy capital's position on this question is almost as ambiguous as it is on incomes policy. Again, the overall position adopted by the CBI and similar national bodies is that 'lame ducks' should not be kept afloat, and that government should impart a spirit of aggressive competitiveness to the economy. In practice, however, a company threatened with bankruptcy or with the need to close a plant will want the government to intervene to help it survive. And if the firm is large enough, and its workers are organized in unions that will themselves lobby Ministers, it stands a good chance of success. Similarly, while industry likes occasional increases in unemployment in order to restrain labour, it also needs a buoyant economy and a good atmosphere of business confidence so that firms can expand.

In general employers want a government which keeps out of industry (but bails out, on industry's terms, firms which get into difficulties); which does not allow the level of unemployment to get too low (but keeps the economy buoyant); which keeps control of trade unions and income growth (but does not get in employers' way when so doing). As stressed here, the position adopted also varies with distance from the national centre. The inability of the centre to co-ordinate the periphery, but corresponding failure of the latter to generate any consistent strategy, is a mark of the irresolute position of British capital as it stands somewhere between liberalism and corporatism. This factor has already been seen in Chapter 5 in the prevarications of Conservative Party policy. Although British industrial capital is now highly concentrated and dependent on government, it has little stomach for corporatism; it does not trust governments always to serve capital's interests, and an organization like the CBI has no power of central co-ordination. At the same time, it cannot return to a true liberal economy, with no trade unions, small competitive industrial units and no need for governments to afford assistance in times of difficulty.

The public sector

It used to be believed by socialists that there would be no industrial relations problems under public ownership. There are certainly differences in the industrial relations practices of the private and public sectors (though few of these are of the kind anticipated), but in general practice within the nationalized industries and government service is as varied as that within privately owned organizations. One major difference between the sectors is that whereas in private industry the main constraint on pay increases is the market, in most of the public sector it is the government's willingness to advance funds. A major dispute in this sector therefore automatically becomes political, however much a government may insist that it is purely a managerial matter. There are contrary theories as to the implications of this politicization, both of which find some support in the facts. The first is that pay in the public sector will be subject to exceptional restraint because a government must apply its own incomes policy to its own employees, whereas in the private sector there will for various reasons be evasions, especially if the policy is not statutory. There is evidence for this in Britain in the late 1950s, the early 1960s (culminating in the postmen's dispute of 1964), and under the 1966 Labour government. The rival theory says that governments are indulgent to their own employees because the public sector contains basic public services where a strike causes massive dislocation for which the government might be blamed, and which can in the short term be solved by the simple expedient of printing more money. There was some support for this interpretation in the early 1970s. It has, however, been argued that the big rises in the public sector in the 1973-5 period were a catching-up process on the preceding years of exceptional restraint in that sector under incomes policy. In an attempt at getting some stability into the collapsing industrial relations system of those years, governments set up various major wage and salary reviews to put pay on an agreed basis. In the public sector these looked at changing relativities over a number of years, and the 'restoration' of public servants' positions resulted in very large increases. This argument applies particularly to the cases of school and college teachers and to civil servants.

Multi-national corporations

An increasing number of companies operating in Britain are multi-national; that is, either British-based companies with extensive overseas branches or foreign companies with branches in Britain.[9] This development has several implications for industrial relations. In some cases foreign firms, particularly American ones, have tried to import their own systems of labour relations, including the exclusion of trade unions; in others they have been innovative in a way that British firms frequently are not –

the Esso productivity agreements described in Chapter 2 were the creation of an American company. But more significant than all these factors is the additional leverage against its labour-force enjoyed by a multi-national corporation. It is not dependent on the workers in any particular country, and if it does not like the unions or industrial relations system it finds there it can move elsewhere. At times this can become a political issue. For example, in 1973 Henry Ford III told the Prime Minister, Edward Heath, that the Ford Motor Company would pull out of Britain if a major dispute at the company was not settled in the corporation's favour. There is less substance in these threats than might initially appear; as proved to be the case with Mr Ford. The huge capital investment of a modern factory cannot just be disposed of at will, and once a firm has established itself in a country it has a considerable stake in remaining there. Of perhaps more substance is the practice of 'double sourcing'. A multi-national firm will ensure that it always has at least two plants, in different countries, producing a particular good or component; if a strike occurs in one country, production is increased of the item in question in the other, and the firm can withstand the strike. Trade unions are beginning to learn that, in order to counter such moves, they will have to develop internationally co-ordinated strikes. But there are formidable obstacles to this and although there have been a few cases of international industrial action, this is an area where capital has a clear advantage.

Where politics as such are concerned, the principal impact of multi-nationals is that a government eager to attract investment may be under pressure to ensure that labour 'behaves itself', because the multi-national can pick and choose where to go. There is as yet little clear evidence whether this has affected British governments. While British industrial relations in the 1970s are generally regarded as having been poor, the same is true of several other Western countries: the USA, Canada, Italy, to a certain extent

France. And while West Germany and Sweden are often held out as having particularly ordered industrial relations, wage levels there are far higher – in fact, Britain stands as an attractively low-wage country in the eyes of many multi-nationals. Far more significant rivalry comes from authoritarian or near-fascist countries where labour is kept down by coercion while wages are also very low: Brazil, Iran, South Korea, South Africa and (until recently) Spain. As the industrial infrastructure of these countries is established and transport problems are solved they will increasingly become, on industrial relations grounds, highly attractive bases for multi-national concerns, with potentially major implications for the politics of industrial relations.

Small-scale capital

While the difference between large and small companies is obviously a matter of degree, there has recently begun to emerge a distinct identity of small-scale firms. This is partly a response to concentration at the other end of the range: the past decade or so has seen an enormous increase in the concentration of British industry, of which the rise of multi-nationals is an important aspect. But the main factor giving a separate identity to small capital concerns the actions of government. Large companies and employers' associations (most of which are dominated by large or middle-sized companies) now exist in close relationship to government, and government interventions in the economy are carried on in close consultation with them. Small firms still live in a largely free-market world, though it is often a market distorted by the relations between state and large companies. Furthermore, small firms are ill equipped to cope with the vast array of taxation, bureaucracy and form-filling which government imposes on companies of all sizes – much of it probably crucial to overall economic success but creating problems for the individual firm. More directly concerned with industrial relations, there has been the spate of recent legislation giving workers increased rights at work, protection from dismissal and rights to compensation in cases of redundancy. Small employers claim that they cannot afford the burden of these provisions or the risk of prosecution in the courts. Further, many of these firms are not unionized or are overtly hostile to unionization. They regard recent legislation giving unions rights to recognition, and the ACAS doctrine of good industrial relations which implies union recognition, as a great threat to their remaining autonomy. Since they constitute one of the few remaining targets for increases in union membership, several of these firms now find themselves the object of union recruitment drives.

All these pressures have led to a new intensity of political activity among small businessmen and the self-employed. They have formed new representative organizations and are refurbishing their existing links with the Conservative Party. (The Labour government has also in fact made important gestures in their direction.) Small firms have also been involved in some lengthy and bitter disputes over union recognition. The Grunwick dispute, discussed in Chapter 4, has so far been the most outstanding case. This is a firm which is really moving out of small-firm status and becoming a middle-sized business, though still being run very much as a one-man show by its founder, George Ward. The firm's resistance was not just directed at its own work-force, their union and the assorted militants who supported them, but against the whole apparatus of modern industrial relations practice – reaching back, in fact, to the entire historically rooted tradition of conciliation. George Ward, in his own account of the Grunwick conflict, describes his struggle as explicitly one against the corporate state.[10] He also makes it clear that in such a struggle a small firm feels isolated, being offered little or no help by the CBI and industry in general.

The main significance of this emerging mood among

small-scale capital is the light it throws on how the structure of the British economy has changed; how there may
soon be a dual economy – with a dominant sector of large,
unionized, publicly and privately owned corporations in
close relationship with government, and a second sector
of small, non-unionized firms standing outside the main
process of economic policy formation. The most immediate political implication has been the effect of small-
business resentment on the Thatcher/Joseph faction, now
dominant, of the Conservative Party. Whether such a
commitment to the priorities of the minority part of the
economy could survive a spell in office by the Conservatives
remains to be seen.

Finance capital and international factors[11]

The British economy has a particularly large financial
sector – banking, insurance, financial services – heavily
oriented to international dealings. This is a legacy of the
nineteenth century, when Britain dominated the capitalist
world and when the pound sterling was the main currency
for international dealings. The significance for industrial
relations of firms in this sector, commonly known as the
City of London, is not primarily as employers of labour.
The vast majority of their workers are white-collar, and
with the exception of the main clearing banks which
accepted the National Union of Bank Employees after a
struggle lasting many years, these firms are hostile to
unionization among their own employees; but their main
importance is in their relation to the rest of the British
economy and its implications.

It is often remarked that the City lacks a representative
organization like the CBI, but to conclude from this that
these institutions have no means of influencing government
policy would be erroneous. The power of the City has rested
primarily in its power over the Treasury (the most important government department), exercised via the Bank

of England and based on the role of sterling in foreign exchange. For most of the post-war period Britain continued its old role of providing, in sterling, one of the capitalist world's two reserve currencies (the other being the US dollar). In the past few years this role has gradually been stripped away, but some of its implications remain. One consequence throughout the period of fixed exchange rates until 1972 was that the City required for its own purposes a high stable value for the currency. At a time when Britain was gradually losing its world economic position this left the country with an overvalued currency. Fears of impending devaluation led to recurrent sterling crises as speculators moved out of the pound until the devaluation might occur; governments were thus faced with an exchange crisis. In order to resolve this they would have to take deflationary action and increase interest rates to tempt money back again. It was in this way that defence of the parity of sterling became the central goal of economic policy before which other goals, such as growth, would from time to time have to be sacrificed, the most notable occasion being in 1966.

But why should the government so repeatedly have accepted the City's priorities, sacrificing expansion and full employment, rather than pursue possible alternatives? After all, the highly successful German economy has entirely lacked a powerful international financial sector of the British kind. First, there has been considerable ambivalence among British governments over the speculative flows of money which the City's work brings. At times of crisis, when money is streaming out, they may find them an appalling nuisance, but the rest of the time, when money is coming and staying in, they provide a useful addition to the country's resources. For example, Britain was temporarily protected from some of the effects of the October 1973 oil crisis by the fact that much of the new Arab oil wealth was channelled through London; the gain was only temporary, the crisis of autumn 1976 being largely the consequence of the sudden rapid withdrawal of these funds.

A further reason for government acceptance of this situation goes to the heart of the source of the City's power. Once a sterling crisis has started, it has potentially very damaging consequences for the economy and it has to be resolved as urgently as possible. The quickest and surest way of doing this is to respond to the demands of the international financial community whose lack of confidence has caused the crisis in the first place; and the main interpreter of these demands and fears is the City, acting through the Bank of England, on which, in turn, the Chancellor of the Exchequer has to rely almost exclusively for policy advice, acting as he is in such situations under the pressure of extreme urgency. Policies which tried to liberate Britain from this straitjacket would, of course, themselves lead to a collapse of international confidence, as overseas holders of sterling would fear that, once this tight network was broken, their demands would no longer be met. It would therefore need a very elaborate, risky and radical set of policies to free the British economy from the vicious spiral of its international financial position, and so far no government has contemplated such possibilities.

The implications of all this for industrial relations lie largely in the short-term horizons and the impossibility of planning which it imposes. If government relations with trade unions are going to be of any use to wage stability, union leaders (not to mention their members) need to have reasonable assurances that if they restrain incomes, certain policies will be pursued which will ensure planned growth in the future. This is, of course, never an easy option, but in an economy which has to be so subordinated to the fluctuations of international finance it is almost impossible. This was important to the collapse of the Labour government's policy of a 'planned growth of incomes' in 1964-6, and again in the inability of the 1974

Labour government to pursue the planning policy which it initially adopted as part of the social contract.

A further important aspect of the City's role is its capacity to act as the transmitter of powerful overseas opinion to British policy-makers in government and industry. As we have seen in this chapter, industrial capital is at something of a loss to discover policies which really suit its interests given free, powerful trade unions – while both low and high unemployment cause it problems. International finance acts without constraint from trade unions or from any other domestic political features. Either it has confidence in an economy and invests in it; or it does not and avoids it – and the presence of a strong trade-union movement may mean that it avoids it. To a certain extent this is a pure market process; the holders of international funds (governments and private groups alike) simply respond in an uncoordinated way to the pattern of risks and opportunities presented to them. But recently, internationally organized sources of capital have become increasingly important, in the shape of such bodies as the International Monetary Fund, the World Bank and, in some ways, the EEC. Whereas the international money market gives signals to governments through market behaviour and through the informal networks of the world's central banks, a body like the IMF makes the process formal. This has appeared most strikingly in Britain since the 1976 crisis; in exchange for the stand-by credit afforded by the Fund, the government has to clear most aspects of economic policy with IMF officials. This, of course, limits the scope for making any agreements on policy with the unions which might offend the interests of international capital.

Britain's highly developed financial system helps channel money away from the country's low-profitability industries into international markets and, domestically, into non-industrial sectors like property. It might be argued that, in the long term, the earnings from these investments will boost British living standards generally, but that is a very uncertain long term.

It may seem surprising that the CBI and other industrial interests have rarely raised any criticism of the role of the City or of the dominance of its major governmental representative, the Treasury. There have been occasions when they might have been close to doing so. For example, in 1964 Harold Wilson deliberately established the Department of Economic Affairs as a counter to the Treasury's predominantly financial interests – the DEA's task being to prepare a national plan for stable growth responsive to the needs of industrial capital. The infant CBI responded fairly warmly to the task. By 1966, however, in the sterling crisis of that year, it was the Treasury's priorities for exchange-rate stability over stable growth that triumphed, and it was not long before the DEA was wound up. Since then the Treasury has kept firm control of economic policy. Apart from isolated individuals, industry raised no protest at this apparent 'victory' for finance capital over industrial capital. Similarly, at the present time the CBI and other industrial lobbies have told the Wilson Commission on financial services that they do not favour any important changes in the structure of the City and its role in investment.

There are primarily two related reasons for this apparent neglect by industrialists of their own interests. First, any move against the City would undoubtedly mean, in the British political context, increased government involvement in investment, probably with a significant trade-union role. Industrialists feel much less threatened by the City, responsive after all to capitalist interests, than by government (especially a Labour one) and union intervention in the issue – investment – that constitutes capital's main power base within society. Second, while it makes sense to separate industrial and financial capital, it is not always easy to allocate individual firms to either category. Many industrial corporations channel their funds through City institutions into the property market or, most important, overseas. In this way they are able to find more immediately profitable outlets for investment and to escape the political context of the UK economy, including its trade unions. Indeed in some years there has been negative investment in British industry by existing firms as they have put their profits into neither their own companies nor other industrial equities but into non-industrial channels. The financial sector thus provides a strategy for capital as a whole, given the lack of room for manoeuvre available to it within domestic industrial relations: escape.

Chapter 7

Labour

Labour is at least as internally differentiated as capital, and the differences between different types of worker are not only those of kind but of hierarchy, denoted by lines of authority, differences in degrees of skill and (largely reflecting these two) systematic inequalities of reward. At the extreme, the gap between an unskilled labourer in casual employment and a senior manager in a giant corporation is vast; does it make any sense to include them both under the category 'labour'? At that extreme, probably not. Top-level managers occupy a position closer to capital than to labour. Even if they are formally responsible to shareholders and count as 'employees', they are not really subject to any authority as such save the discipline of the market – to which capital is nearly always subject anyway. Even their income, though usually taking the form of a salary, is established on a different basis from that of other employees.[1] As one descends the managerial hierarchy, so positions become more ambiguous; in the ranks of middle management are men who spend most of their time organizing and controlling labour, but who are themselves responsible to superiors who, to a certain extent, control their use of their own working time. And while elements of profits-related rewards may be retained in their incomes, they are likely also to be on orthodox salary scales. As one descends even further, to the ranks of junior managerial and supervisory staffs, so one encounters groups who are unambiguously part of labour even if they are carrying on, in Marx's term, 'the labour of superintendence'.

A particular occupation can be included as 'labour' to the extent that the people performing it place themselves at the disposal of an employer who exercises control over the use of their working hours, in exchange for a wage.

To the extent that the work of some employees involves exercising employers' delegated functions there is therefore some ambiguity in their position. This ambiguity is often reflected in the organizations of managerial employees, and the unique position of senior management between labour and capital is seen in the attempt (so far not very successful) by the British Institute of Management to establish itself as an influence on government independent of the CBI and TUC.

The usual ways of classifying various kinds of worker and degrees of skill do not really enable us to make many strong generalizations about differences of interests between different types of labour, since the position varies so much with the issue in question. On a few limited but important matters there is probably a true unity of interest among the whole class of labour; for example, on such demands for employee protection as legislation on unfair dismissal and compensation for redundancy (though employees exercising delegated employer functions may well find irksome the rights that such legislation gives to the workers they are meant to supervise). There may also be a general interest in the reduction of unemployment, though this is probably a priority among manual workers who are more likely to face unemployment – a difference which is perhaps declining as redundancy increasingly encompasses white-collar employees.

It is often argued that there is a fundamental difference between the positions of manual and non-manual workers.[2] Historically there has been, and still is, an important status difference at this point; the two groups have very different working conditions, and in most companies their pay scales are established on a different basis. But this difference should not be exaggerated. There are now several important occupations at the 'technician' level which cannot be easily assimilated to either side of the manual/non-manual line; it is certainly not the case that white-collar workers earn systematically more than manuals; and in a few important cases the traditional distinctions in conditions of employment have been eroded. For purposes of industrial relations it might be best to regard this distinction as one (admittedly important) source of division within the ranks of labour among others. For example, the distinction between skilled, craft-trained workers and the semi-skilled is highly important and has been for many years, as is that between clerical workers and those exercising some kind of professional skill (such as school-teachers or social workers). At the level of day-to-day industrial relations a whole maze of far finer distinctions becomes relevant: small differences in skill level; particular steps in the chain of authority; differences between industries, companies or parts of the country; perhaps differences between workshops of the same company. All these factors may be important in giving particular groups of workers their sense of identity and of entitlements, their capacity to organize; or, more instrumentally, the mere fact that certain differences have in the past been deemed by management to be relevant enables workers to use them to make claims if they would be helpful in so doing. For example, if a firm has traditionally paid one group of workers a certain percentage more than another, the first group will have a *prima facie* case for a rise if the pay of the second group begins to creep up towards them; the workers in question may or may not feel a deep sense of status entitlement, but since in the past there had been an agreed differential and given management's desire to reach consensus on such matters, appeal to the agreement will have considerable force.

All these minute differences and both formal and tacit agreements about relativities are threatened with sudden arbitrary alteration if there is a national incomes policy. It is sometimes claimed that incomes policy helps low-paid workers while free collective bargaining is in the interests of the higher paid, implying an important division of interest within the ranks of labour over the means by which different groups may advance themselves.[8] But the arguments which support this are not very sound; everything depends on the type of incomes policy and the type of collective bargaining involved. First, of course, the 'higher paid' who are helped by bargaining include only those in unionized employment, which tends to exclude most of the very highest paid. Second, it is by no means the case that collective bargaining always favours those whose collective strength is rooted in differentials of skill and responsibility. In the case of unions of the relatively unskilled the whole purpose of organizing will be to try to gain some strength that the workers do not have in their existing market position. Successful wage claims by such groups will tend therefore to reduce differentials between the skilled and the unskilled. Workers on higher rates sometimes also have an interest, admittedly a back-handed one, in raising the pay of lower-paid workers. For example, assume a firm has two factories, one in a high-wage and the other in a low-wage area. The firm will tend to pay lower rates to the latter group, following the wages levels prevailing in the area. If the low-wage group are aware of the difference between their pay and that of their high-wage colleagues they will demand parity. The high-wage factory will probably support them in this, because if the wage differential remains the firm may start transferring work from the high- to the low-wage factory, leading to redundancy among the former group.

Finally, of course, an incomes policy will not necessarily be egalitarian. If the government's intention is simply to maintain stability, it may have a policy of fixed percentage norms (as did incomes policy in the early 1960s), which leaves the existing structure of differentials intact. A more complex policy can incorporate a mixture of goals; for example, the Labour policy, 1965-70, included helping the low paid as a criterion, but gave more attention to the organization of salary structures and the application of comprehensive theories of pay systems which may actually have served to strengthen inequalities. Incomes policy in the 1972-6 period probably had an overall egalitarian impact; it dispensed with the ambitious plans for rational reform to pay structures characteristic of the NBPI and concentrated on largely flat-rate increases with ceilings for the total amount of any rise. This occurred partly because of the severity of the cut-back in real earnings occasioned by the crisis of the mid-1970s, from which governments agreed they had to try to protect the lower paid, and partly because this was a period when the unions were driving a hard bargain for any agreement on restraint, one of their demands being an element of redistribution. In one sense therefore the very strength of collective bargaining led to any egalitarianism which incomes policy possessed.

It is certainly true that the truncation of differentials during certain incomes policies has led to unions breaking their support for the policy. This was the case in 1950, and in 1977 several unions complained of the effect of wage restraint on differentials – a complaint to which the government responded by reverting to a straight percentage base for increases and by acknowledging that various groups whose differentials had been narrowed constituted special cases. This stance by unions, sometimes seeking egalitarian policies and sometimes a restoration of differentials, is not really a contradiction. Given the heterogeneity of the national labour force, it is not surprising that the priorities of different sections come to the fore at different moments. Further, the redistribution which organized labour seeks is usually one from the top of the scale to the middle and bottom, whereas any attempt at putting this into practice will involve redistribution from the middle as well as or instead of the top.

A final problem when considering diversity in the interests of labour concerns relations between labour and consumers. The division is not really one that can be turned into a fundamental social schism, because consumers are simply workers (and their families) in a different guise. While it is often true that, in Harold Wilson's famous phrase, 'One man's wage increase is another man's price increase', the mechanism whereby an increase in the price of labour leads to an increase in the price of the final product is long and indirect. The wage increases of a particular group of workers might be financed at the expense of another group, with no price effect; or it might come from profits, with various possible consequences. The main point is that it is not labour's concern how its increases are financed, because labour is not taken into decision-making on prices.

The issue of labour versus consumers does pose real problems for labour as how best to pursue its own interests, problems which it cannot really solve because it does not itself take decisions over the relevant areas. But the division is sometimes posed much less realistically in terms of unionized versus non-unionized labour. The fact that unions represent little more than half the work-force is often noted. However, where wages are concerned, bargains struck by trade unions are usually extended to the whole industry, whether unionized or not. Further, pay rises negotiated by unions are virtually always extended to the whole work-force in question, and not just those who have joined a union. Further still, if, say, the manual workers in a firm achieve a pay increase it is quite likely that managerial staffs will also receive one because management wants to keep the contours of its pay structure intact. Finally, many firms which are hostile to unions and try to prevent their workers joining them may do so by deliberately paying more than the union-negotiated rate; so in a curious way union bargains fix pay for workers in such firms as well. Another reason for rejecting any fundamental division between unionized and non-unionized labour is that (unlike, say, race) the condition of being non-unionized labour is not immutable; these workers can always join unions, unless of course they face implacable employer opposition.

Divisions within the work-force are therefore many and complex and defy neat generalization. These complications are of considerable importance to any groups trying to promote the interests of labour politically. Of course, to all intents and purposes 'labour' in the political arena means the trade unions, and in particular those unions affiliated to the TUC. It is therefore to them that we should now turn.

Trade unions

Over 50 per cent of the British employed work-force is now unionized – nearly 60 per cent of all male workers and over 65 per cent of male manual workers.[4] Fuller details of membership are given on pages 213-15 in the Appendix. After a period of stagnation in the latter 1950s and early 1960s, union membership has expanded massively. This has been during a period of intensified industrial conflict and, in fact, of increased union unpopularity. One cause of the earlier stagnation had been the inability of unions to re-cruit white-collar workers at a period when their numbers were expanding and those of manual workers declining. This has changed, and women workers, traditionally diffi-cult to organize, have also begun to join unions in greater numbers. The reasons for these developments are beyond the scope of this book, and we simply need to note their implications of growing union strength.

As to different types of trade unions, early this century Sidney and Beatrice Webb drew a threefold distinction which is still of some use: craft unions, general unions and industrial unions.[5] The craft unions were the original trade unions, based on control over recruitment, manning levels and recruitment of workers in skilled, apprenticed trades. The idea of craft skill and the distinctive power of skilled labour remains, though it has a somewhat different mean-ing today. The general unions grew during the last decades of the nineteenth century. These were attempts at organiz-ing workers who had no distinctive skills on which to base their power. Instead they relied on sheer force of num-bers and on recruitment across several different occupa-tions. The TGWU and GMWU are the main inheritors of this tradition. Finally, some unions tried to organize on an industry-wide basis, seeking power by representing all the workers in a particular industry. This was always more an aspiration than a reality – originally an aspiration of the syndicalist movement and more recently of managerialists wishing for a simpler, neater union structure. In only a few areas are there unions that might count as industrial unions – e.g. the Post Office, mining, the steel industry, and even there the craft and technicians unions have an important base. In more recent years a fourth category of unions has been added: those representing white-collar workers.

This classification has its uses, but it does not really work for all British unions. In the past years there has been a wave of union amalgamations, and while this has disposed of many small unions, especially craft unions, it has had the very opposite effect from providing a tidy structure. Instead, large conglomerations spanning the different types have emerged. For example, the AUEW retains its role as a craft union, representing workers with various kinds of engineering skills practised in several industries; within the engineering industry itself it is something of an industrial union; but, the engineering industry being so vast and amorphous, this amounts in effect to being a general union; and it has an important white-collar section. Few unions now have organizational interests in one category alone.

Attempts are sometimes made to draw a sharp distinction between manual and non-manual unions, but few of these stand up to much examination.[6] One relevant difference is that most manual unions are affiliated to the Labour Party while few white-collar unions are. This reflects three factors. First, fewer white-collar workers vote Labour than do manuals, and it would be difficult to get membership agreement to affiliation. Second, while the manual unions grew at a time when the labour movement was struggling to establish itself, and helped sustain the infant Labour Party as part of this effort, the white-collar unions have grown at a time when Labour is already an established party less obviously needing such loyalty. Finally, the majority of white-collar union membership is in the public sector, important sections of which (the civil service, teachers, the professions) feel unable to have a political affiliation.

The majority of trade unions are affiliated to the TUC (which, contrary to popular opinion, is *not* formally attached to the Labour Party). In contrast to most other countries, the TUC has been able to command the allegiance of most white-collar unions within the same confederation as manual unions. This is a fairly recent process. Between 1964 and 1977 NALGO, the National Union of Teachers (and the other teachers' unions), the Association of University Teachers and the Association of First Division Civil Servants, all affiliated, and NALGO is now the fourth largest union in the country. The main reason for this recent success of the TUC is its successful monopoly of channels of communication with government. If a union wants its views expressed it is better off being a member of the TUC, because it then has a route direct to Ministers and senior civil servants. This has happened, not for any inherently political reasons, but because of the general desire of central government (in the interests of convenience and simplicity) to deal with as small a number of different organizations as possible. Just as the various central employers' bodies were persuaded to amalgamate into the CBI, so the TUC has been erected as virtually the sole channel for labour's political demands. Even during the early 1970s, when the conflict over the Industrial Relations Act 1971 brought state-union relations to their lowest ebb, an attempt by various unions and staff associations which had registered under the Act to form an organization with access to Whitehall met with little encouragement from the government. The TUC, which was founded in 1868, used to be a very loose co-ordinating body and its growing power within the union movement has largely been a response to the growing demands of the state.[7] As governments started to intervene in industrial relations and establish incomes policies, they wanted a strong TUC which they could persuade to help them discipline the unions. By the late 1960s, however, the TUC grew further in power as it co-ordinated union *opposition* to incomes policy, and then to the industrial relations legislation attempts of 1969 and 1971. The intensification of tripartite talks since 1972 has entrenched it even more, as have the three Acts of 1974-6; its role within ACAS and the other recent tripartite bodies adds formal elements to the existing important informal role. By the mid-1970s the TUC was acting very much as government had long hoped, as a mediator between it and the unions, as several events described in Chapter 4 have shown.

The unions' political role

British unions stand midway between those of the USA and those of Western European countries in their relationship to politics. The American model is that of 'business unionism', looking after the interests of union members strictly within the employment relationship; most European unions regard themselves as representing the whole working class, and doing so both industrially and politically. Although many US unions do in fact assist the Democratic Party, they regard themselves as politically untied; European unions have usually been the creatures of political parties. Most British unions are affiliated to the Labour Party, but it is of continuing significance that the unions founded the party, and not the other way round. The centre of gravity of the British labour movement is in the workplace, in industrial relations, and this is where its most solid achievements have been won. But the relationship to politics has always been closer than that of American labour. Furthermore, given the greater role of the government in industry in Britain, governments here have demanded more political involvement from unions than has the US government.

The division between industrial and political orientation has been one of the sources of difficulty for unions during the recent period of crisis and state intervention. It is from time to time argued by various interests that the unions would be better off without their political involvements, and that they should turn more thoroughly to a 'business union' model. Conservatives sometimes argue this in an attempt at breaking the Labour Party/union link,[8] but elements in the trade-union left may also argue it, claiming that political loyalties (whether to party or nation) tie the unions' hands in collective bargaining. But it is doubtful whether it is a matter of choice for unions whether they have a political role or not given the contemporary position of the state in industrial relations. Complaints about the unions acting 'politically' usually refer to their occasionally threatening to use industrial power to seek political ends, or to their bias in favour of Labour governments. But it is every bit as 'political' for unions to accept wage restraint in favour of a presumed 'national interest'. In modern society governments have an overriding concern for the state of the economy, and unions' collective bargaining activities have implications for the economy. In such a situation there can be no such thing as pure 'business unionism', even if union leaders, politicians and industrialists wish there could be.[9]

Trade unions thus face a central dilemma. How far can they go in responding to the challenge and opportunities of a political role without sacrificing their primary, bed-rock task of representing their members' immediate interests in improved wages and conditions? It is a dilemma for any union movement, but it is that much more severe if, as in Britain, the unions are in general decentralized and responsive to their members while the state is increasing its economic activities. There are three possible broad paths for unions to take in response to this dilemma: the dogged pursuit of free collective bargaining, asquiescence in government demands, or pursuit of their own autonomous political demands.

The dogged pursuit of collective bargaining is the policy of business unionism already described, where it was shown how this strategy cannot be easily assimilated to either the political right or the left: Conservatives tend to advocate it provided the level of unemployment is high enough to ensure that labour's demands are contained by a non-political process; the union left advocates it on the assumption that unemployment will be low enough to make its demands bite. As with our analysis of industry's positions, there are more systematic variables in terms of distance from the centre, the level of national state-union relations.

Shop-floor activists tend strongly to favour this policy, because it is only at the level of collective bargaining that they have an effective role to play; they do not operate in the political exchange between Ministers and union leaders. The nearer one moves to the centre, the more union representatives are caught up in relations with government, which makes promises and threats to them, creating an environment in which free collective bargaining is not the only option available. The TUC of course stands at the very centre and is the most likely to be diverted from advocacy of free collective bargaining. But this does not mean that union leaders are likely consistently to support some kind of political relationship. Their position is far more cross-pressured than that. As was shown in Chapters 1 and 2, union leaders who neglect their members' immediate interests court disaffection, and their sensitivity to this often leads them to advocate freedom from any political involvement.

Some unions adopt this stance virtually all the time. An example is ASTMS, where a leadership committed to a very left-wing political position combines with a largely non-political, if not Conservative, membership to eschew any interest in pursuing either solidarity with other unions or support for a Labour government. A larger number of unions tends to retreat to advocacy of free collective bargaining, like boxers returning to their corners at the end of a round (in this case, a round of incomes policy). But as the years have gone by, so the rounds have grown longer and the breaks shorter, as was seen in Part One. A spell of unfettered collective bargaining enables union leaders to free themselves from entanglements with government, to avoid facing the awesome problems of national economic policy, to repair relations with their members and to restore differentials distorted by incomes policy. It is unlikely that British unions would ever want to give up the chance of doing this from time to time, and the idea of a permanent incomes policy is probably an illusion. However, the practice of trade unionists and others of regarding free collective bargaining as the 'normal' state of British industrial relations, punctuated at intervals by little bouts of incomes policy, probably needs to be reversed. The pursuit of free collective bargaining has become an occasional and temporary liberation from a norm of incomes policy. It is only by a strange telescopic vision that brings the 1950s closer than the 1960s and 1970s that the former view can be maintained.

If unions are likely to keep returning to free collective bargaining, there are also good reasons for their attempting an important political role instead (or even as well). At present we can postpone the question of whether this political role may be acquiescent or radical.

Union *members* may be presumed to have a primary interest in collective bargaining because it brings about wage increases and other improvements of direct personal benefit to the worker. The union *as an organization* does not, of course, benefit in this way. Rather, it will benefit by extending the scope and power of its activities; by being able to do more things and affect more decisions. Potentially, therefore, unions should be expected to be vulnerable to temptations of a political role, but their willingness to participate in any given case will depend on certain factors. It will increase with the decision-making effectiveness of the forum concerned; thus, unions were able to ignore the National Incomes Commission with few qualms, because it had so few powers. A further factor will be unions' past experience; do they trust government and employers to produce their side of the bargain, in terms of sustained economic or certain social policy goals, if the unions deliver wage restraint? Unions need some basis for trust because they are usually in the position of being asked for wage restraint *now*, so that there might be higher investment *in the future*. The failure of Britain to be able to pursue sustained growth, chronicled in Part One and partly explained in the discussion of finance capital in the previous chapter, must be a relevant factor in explaining unions' wariness of incomes policy commitments. The first phase of the social contract was remarkable in that unions were able to secure their aims, in terms of legislation, in advance of wage restraint, which helps explain their greater commitment to this latest exercise in tripartitism. (It must, however, be pointed out that the unions did not do much about restraint until the government began to hint at sanctions during 1975.) It should also be noted that, at least in the short term, national-level tripartite forums do stand a real chance of reducing inflation. Free collective bargaining does not permit groups to do this for an obvious reason: unilateral restraint by any one group simply leads to its being left behind. Tripartite machinery enables groups to act in concert – assuming, of course, that each group is capable of co-ordinating its members, which is probably true only over the short term.

So far, unions' likely willingness to co-operate with governments has been discussed in general; but it is, of course, highly relevant whether the government is a Labour or Tory one. This does not mean that the unions will do everything they can to help Labour or refuse to co-operate with Conservatives. The various factors already discussed, predisposing both to co-operation and to an inability to take co-operation beyond a certain point, operate all the time, and Part One gave examples of refusal to support Labour policy (in, for example, 1950, 1968-9) and of at least tacit co-operation with the Tories (the early 1950s, and possibly 1972-3). But, at the margin, the ties with Labour often prove decisive.[10] There are all kinds of organizational and patronage links between party and unions; the unions know that they have some control over a Labour government through their supply of finance and votes at party conference; and the pull of traditional and ideological ties may be strong. There is a well-known paradox about this relationship: on the one hand it means that the unions may be able to extract more gains from Labour, but it also means that they are likely to concede more to it.

In the light of all these variables we can work out in which situations unions are or are not likely to acquiesce in government policy. A union with strong Labour Party links (when Labour is in office) and/or accepting the government's definition of the economic situation is likely to be acquiescent if it is also highly centralized and does not have to worry much about membership pressure. This usually means unions with weak memberships and complacent organization; the GMWU and the Union of Shop Distributive and Allied Workers would be examples for much of the period here under review. The ETU (now EET/PU) sometimes comes into this category for rather different reasons concerning the split between 'moderates' and communists in its leadership. The former tend to dominate and try to secure their position by keeping the union in a moderate path and by centralizing its structures, though from time to time they feel the need to take militant steps in order to retain membership loyalty.

A far wider range of unions adopts an acquiescent stance at certain moments. Despite the powerful public image generated by the mining dispute of 1973-4, British unions by and large avoid open confrontation with government. They have established too much strength within existing society lightly to court a plunge into the unknown, especially against the state itself. They are therefore likely to back down from most potential confrontations, often at the expense of assenting to government measures which they dislike. They are also aware that their essential power base, in industry, is not easily translated into political strength which can be wielded against a really determined government. Most of their conflicts with government take the form of threats not to co-operate, or appeals to the trusted traditions of British industrial relations, rather than overt challenges to the authority of the state. As a recent study by M. Moran[11] shows, even the great dispute over the Industrial Relations Act was partly inflamed by the unions' belief that the government had not respected constitutional propriety in framing the Bill.

Various pressures lead unions to take the third option – using their inevitable political involvement to make radical demands, usually as the price of their co-operation. At the most cynical view, unions might demand a price that they know will never be met in order to avoid the obligation to co-operate.[12] Frequently Conservative governments have been told that they cannot expect full co-operation unless they pursue policies of 'social justice'. Since social justice usually means policies associated with the Labour Party, a Conservative administration is unlikely to oblige.

There is some evidence that unions are not just being cynical when they raise these themes. Many people in trade unions, especially the voluntary officials who devote much of their lives to virtually unpaid service, are motivated by political principle and want to extend their activity to the society as a whole and not just to industrial bargaining. More substantially, unions as organizations devoted to wielding power on behalf of their members will welcome a chance to do this in a political forum, seeking gains which cannot be secured by collective bargaining alone. This extension of bargaining to the political sphere has been a dominant feature of the past few years, culminating in the social contract. The issues which can be covered by such bargaining include legal rights for workers, such as protection from unfair dismissal, safety protection or increased public holidays; rights for trade unions themselves; measures for workers' participation in management; a union share in investment decisions; and general social and economic policy measures, such as welfare state reforms, taxation policy and industrial policy. Several examples of such demands were discussed in Part One, especially Chapter 4. Most success has been achieved on the more direct measures – legal rights for workers and unions – while the more far-reaching issues have been honoured more in rhetoric than in practice. Elsewhere I have tried to explain why this is so.[18] While these broad demands are in the interests of the membership, they are so only indirectly or in the long term; in particular, no gains from such demands are experienced in a manner which enables workers to make a direct connection between the union's actions and the outcome. At the same time the union's own interests are also indirect. It gains by the *fact* of participating in forums where it is able to make the demands, though this has to be offset against the restraint on collective bargaining and probable tension with the membership which was the *quid pro quo* for participation; and it is unlikely to achieve much in terms of members' gratitude for any gains. It is particularly doubtful whether unions can wield real industrial strength in pursuit of these wider goals, while the more radical ones would need a considerable marshalling of strength to be successfully gained.

We thus have the paradox of a series of intrinsically important demands being made by unions quite logically and within important national forums, but at the same time not quite seriously. Unions will not stand or fall in the eyes of their members by their performance in these areas, and while demands will be raised and argued about, they are unlikely to be pressed in the way that wage demands are. On the other hand, the more that governments cut off the free collective bargaining option, and the more that bargaining is associated with high inflation from which no one gains, the more unions are likely to have to choose between an acquiescent and a radical political role; and the latter path may be the only way of reconciling union activists to the loss of bargaining autonomy.

In conclusion, then, labour's organizations remain as awkwardly poised between liberalism and corporatism as do the state and most elements of capital. Since both classic economic liberalism and corporatism are strategies for subordinating labour, unions can only gain from contradictions within either system. Thus, a pure liberal economy excludes such organizations as unions; so free collective bargaining, in many respects a highly liberal system, can only thrive once this central element of liberalism has been compromised. Corporatism is in contrast based on organizations, but organizations that are centrally and hierarchically arranged to ensure that labour is disciplined; unions can only gain from corporatism if there are strong elements of organizational autonomy and decentralization, liberal characteristics that contradict corporatism. A full understanding of this situation helps us considerably to understand labour's particular dilemma within the current situation, and to appreciate why what appears to be the unions' considerable power seems capable of being wielded only defensively.

PART THREE

Policy Alternatives and Likely Developments

Chapter 8

Policy Alternatives and Likely Developments

The main alternatives available to Britain in the politics of industrial relations emerge from the analysis in previous chapters. There are two separate choices, each of which opens up two alternatives: are trade unions to remain autonomous, decentralized and powerful, or not? And is the system to develop in a liberal or in a corporatist direction? The available options can be combined to give the following:[1]

Nature of System	Position of Trade Unions	
	Strong	Weak
Liberal	1. Free collective bargaining	2. Neo-*laissez faire*
Corporatist	4. Bargained corporatism	3. Corporatism

As stated in the previous chapter, both liberalism and corporatism can only work in their pure form if labour is subordinated. Under classic economic liberalism, labour is weak because unorganized; under corporatism, it is weak because its organizations are controlled from above and outside. In the table above, the two right-hand boxes constitute the pure models; both left-hand boxes involve compromises with workers' rights to form and control their own powerful organizations. Obviously the different options have very different political and economic implications, and some of these can now be explored.

1. Free collective bargaining

This is the model least likely to dominate in the foreseeable future, though it was the predominant pattern of the 1950s and early 1960s. It is the preferred model of trade unions and especially of the union left. Liberal political economy and strong trade unions being ultimately incompatible, such an option can only survive if there is some external support. A major task of Chapters 1 and 2 was to show how in the post-war period, when free collective bargaining flourished, support was provided, first by a certain element of corporatism arising out of the war-time situation, and second (as that gave way) by growing national prosperity. Now that the particular combination of circumstances which constituted the 'age of affluence' is no longer with us, while the distinctive corporatism of the earlier years ha¯ all but vanished, the free collective bargaining option no longer appears viable. It is always possible that there will be a new advance in national prosperity; the idea of wealth bubbling up out of the sea is, after all (surprisingly), less of a pipe dream than one might in the past have supposed. But even so, this wealth would be coming into a society very different from that of the 1950s. There was then a working class whose historical experience had been two world wars and the biggest recession since the industrial revolution. Prosperity was unexpected and thus, for many people and for several years, in excess of expectations. The working class of the 1980s will be one which takes for granted continual advances in real incomes, as provided in the 1950s, 1960s and indeed much of the 1970s. While there has probably been some check to expectations in the past five years, it is most doubtful whether this would be enough to make people respond as passively as they did during the 1950s and early 1960s. It would need a really spectacular increase in national prosperity fully to absorb popular expectations for an improved standard of living.[2]

In the absence of such unlikely developments, continued free collective bargaining in conditions of trade-union strength is a most uncertain prospect. A condition of union strength is a low overall level of unemployment. (There is just one possible exception to this: a small, unionized sector with low unemployment within a wider economy of weak labour and high unemployment; but this would not be a *system* of free collective bargaining, just islands of it, and anyway in Britain union strength is too evenly distributed throughout the economy for this to be a really likely development.) Now, in the circumstances of the current British and world economies there is no way that free collective bargaining can be maintained alongside full employment without a high rate of inflation. Even if governments are prepared to accept this for a while, international economic forces will soon impose a change of direction; inflation will lead to speculation against the currency, threatening the country's terms of trade and raising the real possibility of economic collapse. This must sooner or later lead to counter-inflationary action. The pattern of events described is not just hypothetical; it is what happened to Britain in 1976.

The government response is almost certain to be action to restrict demand, and this brings unemployment, especially if wages are rising fast. And of course a major consequence of rising unemployment is a check to trade-union strength and thus to the free collective bargaining option itself. Something similar to this happened in West Germany in 1974-5.

There may well be some scope for expanding the economy at the present time; some wage increases may lead to productivity improvements and thus have no effect on prices; or wage rises by some groups may simply be at the expense of other groups, again without an overall price effect. There is therefore some room for manoeuvre in the pursuit of free collective bargaining, but all this is of limited scope. It is sometimes argued by advocates of this option that Britain could insulate itself from international economic forces though protectionist measures, such as import controls and limits on the movement of capital.[3] It may well be that policies of this kind would be in Britain's economic interest; but they would not make unrestrained free collective bargaining a viable policy – rather the reverse. It is inconceivable that a government could control nearly all variables in the economy except wages and salaries, for this could only mean high inflation.

Inflation is not necessarily the ultimate economic evil that must be avoided at all costs; a certain rate of inflation may be more acceptable to many people than the consequences of certain policies for controlling it, such as very high unemployment or the suspension of certain basic freedoms.[4] But there is considerable debate over the conditions under which inflation can be contained at relatively low levels. Once it reaches those levels experienced in Britain and elsewhere in the wake of the oil crisis of the mid-1970s, it is doubtful whether anyone is content with it – and as far as collective bargaining is concerned, all it does is erode its achievements. It is therefore naïve in the extreme to pretend that a return to unrestrained collective bargaining alongside full employment is a viable option in itself. Unions may want to retain the *threat* of trying to return to it, in order to strengthen their bargaining position under some of the other options, and that is a sound enough strategy. And shop-floor workers may well advocate it on the grounds that it is only at that level that they can affect anything, while they are in no position to control the economy as a whole – an understandable position, some of the implications of which will be considered below. Finally, some groups may advocate this option not because they believe in it as such but because they believe it will hasten the collapse of the Western economic system, from which they expect a new social order to arise. To adopt such a position is to express a confidence in the human capacity to extract something good out of chaos and disarray which many will find rather unconvincing, especially in the light of twentieth-century history.

2. Neo-*laissez faire*

There are superficial resemblances between free collective bargaining and this second option. Some Conservatives join such figures of the union left as Arthur Scargill, leader of the Yorkshire miners, in calling for the government to keep out of relations between employers and workers. The difference is that while the union left assumes a government commitment to full employment, Conservatives would regulate demand so that wage increases beyond those which the market would have anyway provided lead directly to unemployment. This would be achieved by tight control of the money supply and the regulation of public spending. This is not advocacy of free collective bargaining in any commonly understood sense.

Involved is not just a policy of demand control. There would also be tax cuts and a reduction in public spending (apart from the armed forces and police, where expenditure would be increased). It could be that reductions in taxation would have some effect in limiting wage demands; in Chapter 4 the activities of the 1974 Labour government in this area were discussed and explained. This might provide something of a dilemma for the unions, given not only their long-term political commitment to public spending on the social services but also the considerable weight of public-sector unions who have a clear and obvious interest in a high level of public expenditure. It is in fact unlikely that unions would be happy with such a situation, while public spending cuts would bring conflict in other areas of society over deteriorating education, health services, roads and housing conditions.

It is further claimed for the neo-*laissez faire* option that tax cuts, increased social inequality and a reduction in government intervention would liberate enterprise, leading to greatly increased prosperity for all and, in the long run, the chances of true free collective bargaining combined with low unemployment, as in the first option.[5] The doubts that exist over the capacity for prosperity again to have the implications it did in the 1950s have already been expressed. More generally, the chain of reasoning that starts with tax cuts and ends with a great increase in economic growth stemming from released entrepreneurial energies involves several very large and untestable assumptions, and, in its unsubstantiated optimism, does not fall very far short of the argument that high inflation might lead, via chaos, to a new social order.

However, a major strength of this option lies in the support it enjoys from international and finance capital. A continuing problem for *laissez faire* is that it has to try to put economic decisions beyond the reach of democratic politics – not beyond *all* politics, because it will be important that government takes political measures necessary to sustain the *laissez faire* system, but beyond democratic pressures for full employment and social services. Several advocates of this strategy have therefore spoken of the need to roll back democracy, or to elevate some institution, such as the central bank, which cannot be 'interfered with' by politics.[6] To some extent finance capital and the international monetary system provide such a possibility. It emerged from the discussion in Chapter 6 that these are the only sectors of capital which have a fairly clear means of avoiding compromise and pressure from labour. Finance capital can move at will between countries, rejecting those with strong labour movements, and it does not get bogged down in the horse-trading of either collective bargaining or tripartitism which is the lot of industrial capital. Furthermore, democracy and trade unions do not operate internationally. A government dependent on international capital will therefore be subject to strong pressures to withstand domestic labour pressure. The recent role of the IMF in the British economy provides a very clear instance of how this operates.

Neo-*laissez faire* is therefore a major force to reckon with as a likely future development, but it has distincts costs and certain snags. The continued high unemployment on which it depends in the short and possibly medium term means postponing for some time any real recovery of the British industrial economy. And as recovery eventually began there would be a particular tricky moment, with unions realizing their strength was increasing and workers eager to make up for the deprivations of the years of recession at a time before the economy was in fact in a position to produce widespread new wealth. This is a highly vulnerable moment for an economy which is restraining collective bargaining through demand management alone, and it could well result in continued postponement of the recovery. Furthermore, the strongest groups in the labour market are among the least likely to be hit by unemployment. Union strength being high among skilled workers whose work is vital to the economy – for example, miners, power engineers, certain sectors of engineering – unions are likely to continue to be powerful at certain crucial points. One of three courses of action must be pursued: (i) constant concessions would have to be made to these groups (as has in fact been advocated by some Conservatives), leading to distortions in the labour market and considerable resentment elsewhere; (ii) unemployment would have to bite very deep indeed in order to affect even these groups; or (iii) there would have to be considerable coercion, using the police and the armed forces, to break strikes in these powerful sectors.

Overall, the *laissez faire* option means pushing back trade-union strength by means other than compromises and agreements, neutralizing various democratic pressures on economic policy and cutting back severely on public services. That *laissez faire* was not a matter of economic policy alone was recognized by the Conservative Party when it last adopted a stance of this kind in the late 1960s, as outlined in Chapter 3. The machinery then advocated for buttressing economic by political control was legislation of the kind that eventually became the Industrial Relations Act, combining a degree of corporatism with straightforward legal limitation of trade-union freedoms. In the light of the experience of that Act the emphasis has now shifted. Strict demand regulation would now be accompanied by some kind of corporatist understanding with the unions and/or a new emphasis on the role of the police and the army.

Both aspects of this new emphasis are paradoxical. One of the purposes of neo-*laissez faire* is, according to its advocates, to stop the growth of corporatism; the possibility that it may in fact be *dependent* on corporatist strategies will be considered below. Reliance on police and army may seem paradoxical in that a party which stresses its dedication to freedom, and opposition to state interference finds itself, precisely as a result of having dismantled means of government intervention, relying more on the most coercive and least democratically responsible arms of the state. The paradox is not the result of any muddled thinking among contemporary Conservatives; it lies deep in the classic liberal model of the state. Economic liberalism does not imply a weak state; it is merely opposed to detailed government interference with the rights of property owners, and if the cost of doing that is considerable interference with other kinds of liberty, then so be it. It is very important to grasp this point, and in particular not to label the exercise of just any kind of state power as corporatist.

3. Corporatism

There have been distinct signs of corporatist developments in Britain, as has been discussed in previous chapters. But these have had very limited success, because the base for corporatism within British society is poorly developed owing to the strength of the liberal legacy. The trade-union movement is very decentralized, with strong shop-floor roots; civil liberties are deeply entrenched; industrial organizations like the CBI have few powers of co-ordination; the financial sector is large, powerful and external to the structure of organized interests; there is a strong sense of the autonomy of society from the state; and there has been a decline in social and moral cohesion. These characteristics of Britain emerge from any comparison between it and those countries in which corporatism of various kinds has been more prominent – such as West Germany, Japan, Sweden and the Netherlands.[7] On the other hand, in a comparison with such countries as France or Italy[8] one is struck by certain features favourable to corporatism: the long-standing unity of the nation; a certain surviving legacy of cohesion from the 1940s; and a much more recent acceleration in the pace of organization of economic interests. The United Kingdom is thus interestingly poised between various kinds of liberal and corporatist elements. In recent years this balance has mainly taken the form of corporatist attempts; but there have been few successes, an important stumbling block being the continuing strength of organized labour.

Corporatism and *laissez faire* are opposed models of social organization, and in some respects they constitute the main political alternatives being 'offered' to Britain at the present time. However, as has already been hinted, they may now actually be complementary. An example has been Britain since 1976; a combination of monetarism with more or less co-operative trade unions offering wage restraint. This alliance can be explained in terms of the position of labour. Where there is a strong labour movement, a liberal economy cannot work because labour's power goes beyond the purely economic, so corporatist measures are introduced to regulate labour at the level of organizations. But how is this possible if labour has such a high degree of autonomous strength? By weakening that strength through high unemployment and monetarism.

This is the important fact overlooked by those advocates of neo-*laissez faire* who see themselves as opposed to the corporate state. A distinct pattern is emerging in the Western world, of domestic corporatism disciplined by international monetarism.[9] The UK and West Germany are probably the most outstanding cases, but there have been notable attempts in Italy, the Netherlands and elsewhere. If Keynesianism characterized much of the post-war world, this new combination seems to characterize the political economy of the late 1970s. It may well be 'successful' in controlling inflation, but it is a rather unattractive option, combining the restrictions of both economic liberalism and corporatism without the compensating attractions of either. There is also some doubt over how long it could last, largely because of characteristics of the union movement which will now be considered further.

4. Bargained corporatism

As is argued in a recent study[10] of the West German trade-union movement – probably the most co-operative in Western Europe – no trade union can co-operate indefinitely with employers and government without doing something to represent its members' immediate interests, at least not in a free society. In fascist and communist countries where non-co-operative unions can be liquidated and membership of co-operative ones made compulsory, the same rule might not apply, though even there unions probably have to play some role in limited grievance representation in order to stem the development of incipient rival channels. The problem is that unions will become unable to deliver their members' consent to restraint if they never offer them anything to make acceptance of co-ordination by the union leadership worthwhile. Legal sanctions imposing certain kinds of discipline over workers who act outside formal union channels may alleviate this difficulty to some extent;

the German legal system does so at several points, the Industrial Relations Act tried unsuccessfully to do so in Britain. But this kind of compulsion, even if it can be introduced, is unlikely completely to relieve representative organizations of the need to represent. The consequence of this is a continual slippage away from corporatist arrangements to free collective bargaining on the part of union leaderships. This means that union consent to participation in corporatist relations has to be continually regained by governments through concessions – either concessions to compensate unions for the difficult time they will have at the hands of their members, or concessions that will be experienced as such by the members. This makes possible what I have elsewhere described as 'bargained corporatism': [11]

> It involves acceptance by unions of several strategies which, compared with liberal collectivism [free collective bargaining], constitute a set-back for [workers'] interests. But it also holds out the chance of advances. Unions are tempted – and frightened – by corporatist developments to sacrifice some of their entrenched but narrow and unambitious achievements in exchange for the possibility of greater political influence and more and broader power for their members in the work-place, but at the same time to accept more restraint, a more obvious role for the unions in restraining their members, more state interference and fuller acceptance of the industrial order and its priorities.

The possibility of unions undertaking this kind of bargaining in exchange for their commitments under corporatism opens up a chink of light in what is otherwise a tight, closed system. Unions accept periods of wage restraint, the relaxation of protective practices and similar measures, in the interests of improving efficiency; but on the conditions that they receive in return (i) certain other gains for their members and themselves and (ii) a share in making the economic policy of which the efficiency measures are a part. The former opens up interesting possibilities. In incomes policy the government interposes itself between the unions and their normal bargaining partner, the employer, but in so doing becomes itself their bargaining partner; and the government is able to offer several things which cannot be achieved in bargaining – and which may be less self-defeating than wage claims often are – such as social policy reforms, workers' rights, changes in economic and fiscal policy. A share in making economic policy is necessary if unions are to have any genuine confidence that the restraints and concessions which they offer are necessary and are being matched by changes elsewhere in society for the same ends of efficiency.

These possibilities raise several difficult problems. First, there is the relationship between the emerging political role of unions and employers' organizations and that of parliament. Historically, parliament has been associated with liberal political economy, which minimizes the role of organized economic interests. In his recent study, M. Moran[12] shows effectively how Conservatives have come to believe that they are at a disadvantage in this kind of interest representation; as a result, they are both loud in their advocacy of the central role of parliament and of monetarism as the only economic policy which might (though not according to the arguments I have developed here) free the state from economic activity. (It should be noted that the 'sovereignty of parliament' refers only to its relationship to certain, that is labour, pressures; closely allied to monetarism is the idea of the central bank being autonomous and thus *not* subordinate to parliament.) As Moran points out, Conservatives have also turned their minds to an alternative to parliament which would serve the real aim, which is to reduce the political weight of unions. This is the idea of the plebiscite, or referendum, perhaps to be used during a major national strike in order to wield public opinion against the unions. The strategy is presumably based on the fairly sound grounds that, since

Conservative interests have effective control over mass communications, they are more likely to succeed through a populist appeal than by trying to come to terms with organized interests.

En route, Conservatives find themselves jettisoning a very weighty old Tory doctrine about the importance of government working in harmony with the great vested interests of the society, which has curiously become a Labour Party doctrine instead.[18] On the other hand quasi-corporatist organization is very vulnerable to criticism. Unlike parliament, it is based on no universal representation comparable to 'one man, one vote', and there are real possibilities of whole sections of the community being left out of consideration. However, this does not in practice follow as automatically as might seem to be the case in theory. For example, Moran cites retirement pensioners as a group which parliament will care for but which will be left out of account in state-union bargaining. In reality, pensioners in Britain, long neglected by parliament, have seen a major improvement in their relative income position since the trade unions adopted their cause when bargaining with government (largely, but not entirely, through the personal concern of Jack Jones).

The issue is not a simple one. Of course, if one believes that parliament is the effective decision-making body of our national affairs, or that it is only prevented from being so by the power of trade unions, then one can adopt a clear-cut view. If, on the other hand, one sees the management of a modern economy, with its inevitably organized interests, as something which will always be beyond the control of parliament, and which will be controlled through the interchange of government bureaucracy, international monetary institutions and domestic organized interests, then one may well come to see the scope for some autonomous action by the unions within that framework as the best hope for an element of pluralism in our emerging political economy. One weakness of recent developments has been their *ad hoc* nature, and eventually there would need to be some established institutional embodiment. However, it is premature to try, as some have recently done, to follow the Webbs in drawing up blueprints for an 'industrial parliament' or similar body. For the time being it is best that governments, unions, employers and everybody else become practised in and accustomed to the substance of the process, working out its possibilities and limitations. In many areas of policy this country has recently had a surfeit of institutional innovation, of attempts at solving deep-seated problems by the creation of empty, cosmetic (and often expensive and bureaucratic) formal bodies as substitutes for real answers.

A second and probably greater problem recalls certain problems outlined in Chapter 7: often the issues which might be up for negotiation are of little interest to unions' shop-floor members, because ordinary workers have little opportunity to affect anything beyond their own money wage and therefore cannot be expected to perform as though they were actors on any wider stage. It is at this point that several observers have developed the case for a major increase in workers' participation. If shop stewards are to be expected to act in some wider company – or even national – interest in their activities, then they must be able to share fully in decision-making at the company level, and through their unions be closely involved in problems of national economic policy-making; and, it might be added, it will no longer be adequate for companies to be legally limited to the protection of shareholders' interests alone, with workers regarded as simply one of the commodities which the company uses. It is thinking along these lines which has generated, with different degrees of radicalism, the British Leyland and Chrysler participation experiments, the Bullock Report and wider plans for giving unions a say in the investment decisions of financial institutions (especially of their members' insurance funds). It is all very well telling workers that their actions will threaten investment and the position of the firm, but how do they know all this to be true unless their representatives are involved in the relevant decision-making? Employers resort to bluff and exaggeration frequently enough for scepticism to be justified.

It is usually employers' representatives who bemoan the idea of 'two sides of industry' and who call upon workers to co-operate in the common good. But it was not workers who instituted the rigorous distinction between those who make decisions and those who receive instructions. Or, to put it another way, how can responsibility be demanded from those to whom responsibility is not given? The changes needed to induce more co-operation in British industry will have to be at the level of power and structure before they can be expected in workers' attitudes.[14] The same might not be true in countries with a less well developed, less decentralized trade-union movement; it might then be possible for deals and understandings between capital and labour to be limited, on the labour side, to the leaders of formal organizations rather than to the workers themselves. Such was the case in Britain from about 1940 until 1950, and again over the past few years. But it could have no permanency unless something were to be done to destroy finally the base of shop-floor power. The achievement of this task would involve a major interference with both democracy and liberty.

Those who reject such a course of action, but who also realize the futility of labour persisting with the pursuit of free collective bargaining as its chief end in life, must take seriously the implications of the bargained corporatism option. Superficially, it seems a convenient compromise, half-way between collective bargaining and the incorporation of unions, and in some senses it would constitute yet another compromise between the forces of order and freedom, or between capital and labour. But it is not a compromise in the same sense of being the easy way out, the line of least resistance. To be really serious about labour being in a position to bargain knowledgeably about the terms on which it would offer collaboration in the pursuit of efficiency means to contemplate radical changes, not just at the national political level, but also within industry. It means, for example, the extension of industrial democracy on lines at least as radical as the Bullock majority report. At the industrial level it means a major extension of the economic development committee system within NEDC, so that unions are technically equipped to engage in a debate about real planning with the employers, leading to the negotiated introduction of agreed changes. This may not seem too remote a possibility, but it is problematic. Such an extension of unions' activity would involve the growth of their own expert officialdom, working on technical tasks of industrial development, probably at the expense of more direct services to members. Some German unions are beginning to experience this problem. It could only be overcome if the unions were able to involve and interest shop-floor activists in such issues; this would not be easy, though it would be less difficult once a system of industrial democracy.

A further problem of all these reforms would occur if Britain were to move in this direction in isolation – though whether it would in fact be doing so is another matter. Earlier chapters have drawn attention to the international constraints imposed on our political economy at the present time. The warnings sounded by the CBI as to the likely implications for overseas investment in this country if the government had gone ahead with Bullock may be taken as a reliable guide to the response which other similar moves would invoke. In the foreseeable future there is going to be some competition in attracting investment between, on the one hand, all those countries professing a degree of ordinary democracy and, on the the other hand, such nations as Brazil, South Africa, South Korea and possibly eventually Iran and Saudi Arabia, which are able to offer capital an environment less threatened by civil rights and freedoms. The position of a country extending democracy further into the industrial arena would be more vulnerable still. All this indicates further implications of bargained corporatism, in terms of policy on freedom of capital movements and on the international co-ordination of labour-movement policies – to date, not an area boasting of impressive achievements.

As this brief review indicates, bargained corporatism taken seriously is uncomfortably uncertain and radical. But to set against these points which may seem to remove it from the area of reality is the fact that, at the more humble levels, several developments identifiable as part of bargained corporatism have begun to occur, in Britain and elsewhere. First and foremost, there has been the need to offer unions something at the national political level in exchange for restraint. The extension of workers' rights at work, and various fiscal changes of the past few years would probably not have occurred if governments had not been engaged in this bargaining process, and they did not occur during earlier phases of incomes policy. Similarly, the discussion with union leadership of major parameters of the country's economic development by governments and the CBI has been extended considerably since the foundation of the NEDC in 1962 and especially since Edward Heath's programme of tripartite talks ten years later. At the level of individual industries or large companies there are now many cases of shop stewards being taken into some kind of confidence over investment plans, and (sometimes as part of the same process) major new experiments in industrial democracy.

How likely is it that these openings will develop into the more radical possibilities? It is my view that further developments along the lines of bargained corporatism constitute the most attractive opportunities presented to this country by the recent turmoil around industrial relations, offering chances for the extension of real democracy in the management of economic affairs which has always eluded us. But overall, as perhaps the above discussion of obstacles has suggested, I am not optimistic about the capacity of British institutions to achieve changes of this order. Some combination of monetarism and attempts at straightforward corporatism are more likely to be the order of the day; in which case occasional union bargaining triumphs for shop-steward consultation over investment plans, or for reforms in some area of social policy in exchange for a limited programme of wage restraint, are likely to be the most encouraging outcomes that we can expect,

Notes on the Text

Chapter 1: The Post-war Period

For further reading on this period see the following works, on which this chapter has drawn freely: V. L. Allen, *Trade Unions and the Government* (London: Longmans, 1960); H. A. Clegg, *The System of Industrial Relations in Great Britain*, third edition (Oxford: Blackwell, 1977); G. A. Dorfman, *Wage Politics in Britain 1945-1967* (Ames: Iowa University Press, 1973); L. Panitch, *Social Democracy and Industrial Militancy* (Cambridge: at the University Press, 1976); E. H. Phelps Brown, *The Growth of British Industrial Relations* (London: Macmillan, 1959); B. C. Roberts, *National Wages Policy in War and Peace* (London: Allen and Unwin, 1958).

1. For more details see M. Stewart, *Keynes and After* (Harmondsworth: Penguin, 1967).
2. Details will be found in Allen, *op. cit.*
3. For a biography of Bevin, see A. Bullock, *The Life and Times of Ernest Bevin*, Volumes I and II (London: Heinemann, 1960 and 1969).
4. But, characteristically of British politics, it did not even then press its victory as far as it might. As the Conservative Prime Minister at the time, Stanley Baldwin, put it: '. . . we are going to withdraw our hand; we are not going to push our political advantage home. Although I know that there are those who work for different ends from most of us in this House, yet there are many in all ranks and in all parties who will re-echo my prayer: "Give Peace in our time, O Lord."' (Quoted in A. H. Halsey, *Change in British Society* [Oxford: at the University Press, 1978] pp. 70-1.)

5. For a wider discussion, see K. W. Wedderburn, *The Worker and the Law*, second edition (Harmondsworth: Penguin, 1971); and O. Kahn-Freund, 'Labour Law', in M. Ginsberg (ed.), *Law and Opinion in England in the Twentieth Century* (London: Stevens, 1959).

6. For an account of the incomes policy of the late 1940s, see B. C. Roberts, *op. cit.*

7. For a popular history of the Ministry of Labour, see E. Wigham, *Strikes and the Government* (London: Macmillan, 1975).

8. Cmnd 9725 (London: HMSO, 1956).

9. A full account of these disputes and their implications will be found in H. A. Clegg and R. Adams, *The Employers' Challenge* (Oxford: Blackwell, 1957).

10. Both disputes are discussed in Allen, *op. cit.*

Chapter 2: Years of Growing Tension

For further reading on this period see the following works, on which this chapter has drawn freely: H. A. Clegg, *The System of Industrial Relations in Great Britain*, third edition (Oxford: Blackwell, 1977); C. J. Crouch, *Class Conflict and the Industrial Relations Crisis* (London: Heinemann, 1977); G. A. Dorfman, *Wage Politics in Britain 1945-1967* (Ames: Iowa University Press, 1973); L. Panitch, *Social Democracy and Industrial Militancy* (Cambridge: at the University Press, 1976); I. Richter, *Political Purpose in Trade Unions* (London: Allen and Unwin, 1973).

1. For a detailed analysis of strike statistics, see M. Silver, 'Recent British Strike Trends: a Factual Analysis', *British Journal of Industrial Relations*, March 1973.

2. For an account, see C. H. Rolph, *All Those in Favour* (Harmondsworth: Penguin, 1961).

3. W. Fellner, *Policies for Price Stability* (Paris: OEEC,

1961). For a general account of the move towards planning, see A. Budd, *The Politics of Economic Planning* (London: Fontana, 1978); and J. Leruez, *Economic Planning and Politics in Britain* (London: Martin Robertson, 1976).

4. Dorfman, *op. cit.*, gives more details of the politics of negotiating the establishment of NIC and NEDC.

5. Leruez, *op. cit.*, p. 243.

6. For an analysis of the Commission's work, see Crouch, *op. cit.*

7. K. W. Wedderburn, *The Worker and The Law*, second edition (Harmondsworth: Penguin, 1971) provides an analysis of the case, together with others like it in subsequent years, and discusses its implications for industrial relations.

8. More details of the establishment and functions of the NBPI will be found in Crouch, *op. cit.*

9. M. Stewart, *The Jekyll and Hyde Years: Politics and Economic Policy since 1964* (London: Dent, 1977) provides an analysis of economic policy decisions, together with rejected options, from this period to the mid-1970s.

10. For fuller accounts see Crouch, *op. cit.*; *idem*, 'The Ideology of a Managerial Elite: the National Board for Prices and Incomes', in I. Crewe (ed.), *The British Political Sociology Yearbook*, Volume I: *Elites in Western Democracy* (London: Croom Helm, 1974); *idem*, 'The Drive for Equality? The Experience of Incomes Policy in Britain', in L. N. Lindberg *et al.* (eds.), *Stress and Contradiction in Modern Capitalism* (Lexington: D. C. Heath, 1975); A. Fels, *The British Prices and Incomes Board* (Cambridge: at the University Press, 1972); J. Mitchell, *The National Board for Prices and Incomes* (London: Secker and Warburg, 1972).

11. In its various general reports: Cmnd 3087 (1966); Cmnd 3394 (1967); Cmnd 3715 (1968); Cmnd 4130 (1969); Cmnd 4649 (1971).

12. S. Brittan and P. Lilley, *The Delusion of Incomes Policy* (London: Temple Smith, 1977).
13. NBPI, Report No. 36, *Productivity Agreements*, Cmnd 3311 (London: HMSO, 1967).
14. *The Fawley Productivity Agreements* (London: Faber and Faber, 1964).
15. See C. J. Crouch, 'The Intensification of Industrial Conflict in the United Kingdom', in *idem* and A. Pizzorno (eds.), *The Resurgence of Class Conflict in Western Europe since 1968*, Volume I: *National Studies* (London: Macmillan, 1978).

Chapter 3: The Collapse of the Post-war System

For further reading on this period see the following works, on which this chapter has drawn freely: C. J. Crouch, *Class Conflict and the Industrial Relations Crisis* (London: Heinemann, 1977); *idem*, 'The Intensification of Industrial Conflict in the United Kingdom', in *idem* and A. Pizzorno (eds.), *The Resurgence of Class Conflict in Western Europe since 1968*, Volume I: *National Studies* (London: Macmillan, 1978); M. Moran, *The Politics of Industrial Relations* (London: Macmillan, 1977); L. Panitch, *Social Democracy and Industrial Militancy* (Cambridge: at the University Press, 1976); E. Wigham, *Strikes and the Government 1893-1974* (London: Macmillan, 1976).

1. All three were fellows of Nuffield College, Oxford.
2. *Report* of the Royal Commission on Trade Unions and Employers Associations, Cmnd 3623 (London: HMSO, 1968). The Commission's research reports, its minutes of evidence and the written evidence of the more important witnesses are also published by HMSO. For a detailed analysis of the evidence and the Report, see Crouch, 1977, *op. cit.*
3. Cmnd 3888 (London: HMSO, 1969).

4. A full account of all these negotiations is given in P. Jenkins, *The Battle of Downing Street* (London: Knight, 1969).
5. For more details of the parliamentary conflict, especially the role of the Trade Union Group of MPs, see J. Ellis and R. W. Johnson, *Members from the Unions* (London: Fabian Society, 1974).
6. On the upsurge of militancy since the late 1960s, including details of the groups involved and the development of new tactics of action, see Crouch, 1978, *op. cit.*
7. M. Silver, 'Recent British Strike Trends: a Factual Analysis', *British Journal of Industrial Relations*, March 1973.
8. For more details on the content and implications of the Industrial Relations Act, see Crouch, 1977, *op. cit.*; for a full account of the conflicts surrounding its preparation and subsequent implementation, see Moran, *op cit.*
9. This is discussed in particular detail in Moran, *ibid.*
10. For an account by one of those involved, see E. Heffer, *The Class Struggle in Parliament* (London: Gollancz, 1971).
11. This and the following accounts of the operation of the Act have drawn heavily on B. Weekes, M. Mellish, L. Dickens and J. Lloyd, *Industrial Relations and the Limits of Law* (Oxford: Blackwell, 1975).
12. For further details, see D. Butler and D. Kavanagh, *The British General Election of February 1974* (London: Macmillan, 1974).
13. Crouch, 1977, *op. cit.*, pp. 247, 248.

Chapter 4: Picking up the Pieces

This chapter has drawn heavily on C. J. Crouch, *Class Conflict and the Industrial Relations Crisis* (London: Heinemann, 1977); *idem*, 'The Intensification of Industrial

Conflict in the United Kingdom', in *idem* and A. Pizzorno (eds.), *The Resurgence of Class Conflict in Western Europe since 1968*, Volume I: *National Studies* (London: Macmillan, 1978); J. Elliott, *Conflict or Co-operation?* The *Growth of Industrial Democracy* (London: Kogan Page, 1978); and the regular 'Chronicle' of events recorded in the *British Journal of Industrial Relations*.

1. Crouch, 1977, *op. cit.*, p. 185.
2. Cmnd 6151 (London: HMSO, 1975).
3. F. Wilkinson and H. A. Turner, 'The Wage-Tax Spiral and Labour Militancy', in D. Jackson *et al.*, *Do Trade Unions Cause Inflation?*, second edition (Cambridge: at the University Press, 1975).
4. These developments are discussed in more detail in Chapter 7.
5. The number of bankruptcies rose from 3380 in 1973 to 6700 in 1976 (Department of Trade, *Bankruptcy: General Annual Report for 1977* [London: HMSO, 1978].
6. For a detailed account of the circumstances, substance and implications of the Bullock Committee and its Report, see Elliott, *op. cit.*
7. Subsequently, however, there have been two important studies of the experiment: one, critical and sceptical, is P. Brannen, E. Batstone, D. Fatchett and P. White, *The Worker Directors: a Sociology of Participation* (London: Hutchinson, 1976); the other, a rejoinder, is British Steel Corporation Employee Directors with J. Banks and K. Jones, *Worker Directors Speak* (Farnborough: Gower, 1977).
8. Interim and Final Reports on Industrial Democracy (London: TUC, 1973 and 1974 respectively).
9. Elliott, *op. cit.*, p. 245.
10. *Industrial Democracy*, Cmnd 7231 (London: HMSO, 1978).
11. A detailed account of both the dispute and its implications is J. Rogaly, *Grunwick* (Harmondsworth: Pen-

guin, 1977). Obviously less objective, but highly interesting, is the account of the employer himself, George Ward, *Fort Grunwick* (London: Temple Smith, 1977).

Chapter 5: The State

1. London: Heinemann, 1977.
2. C. B. MacPherson, *The Political Theory of Possessive Individualism* (Oxford: Clarendon Press, 1962).
3. For a famous account of its demise, see S. Dangerfield, *The Strange Death of Liberal England* (London: Constable, 1936).
4. There are several accounts of this, a standard work being H. Pelling, *A History of British Trade Unionism* (Harmondsworth: Penguin, 1971).
5. P. C. Schmitter, 'Still the Century of Corporatism?', *Review of Politics*, 36, 1, 1974; *idem*, 'Modes of Interest Intermediation and Models of Societal Change in Western Europe', *Comparative Political Studies*, 10, 1, 1977; and C. J. Crouch, *op. cit.*
6. K. Yamamura, 'A Marriage in Middle Years: a Politico-Economic Analysis of Japanese Inflation', in L. N. Lindberg and C. S. Maier (eds.), *The Politics and Sociology of Global Inflation and Recession* (Washington DC: Brookings Institution, forthcoming).
7. For further details of certain European countries, see C. J. Crouch and A. Pizzorno (eds.), *The Resurgence of Class Conflict in Western Europe since 1968*, two volumes (London: Macmillan, 1978).
8. H. A. Clegg, *How to Run an Incomes Policy and Why We Made such a Mess of the Last One* (Harmondsworth: Penguin, 1972); S. Brittan and P. Lilley, *The Delusion of Incomes Policy* (London: Temple Smith, 1977).
9. For an account concentrating on the Conservative Party, see N. Harris, *Competition and the Corporate Society* (London: Methuen, 1972); for one concentrat-

ing on Labour, see L. Panitch, *Social Democracy and Industrial Militancy* (Cambridge: at the University Press, 1976).

10. London: Fontana, 1977. See also K. W. Wedderburn, *The Worker and The Law* (Harmondsworth: Penguin, 1971).

Chapter 6: Capital

1. The different positions of different sections of capital on industrial relations questions are discussed in detail in D. Strinati, 'Capitalism, the State and Industrial Relations', in C. J. Crouch (ed.), *State and Economy in Capitalist Society* (London: Croom Helm, forthcoming).

2. V. G. Munns and W. E. J. McCarthy, *Employers' Associations*, Donovan Commission Research Paper No. 7 (London: HMSO, 1967) is one of the few works on the role of employers' associations.

3. See S. Blank, *Government and Industry in Britain* (Farnborough: Saxon House, 1973) for an account of the political role of the FBI.

4. A recent comprehensive account of the CBI is W. Grant and D. Marsh, *The CBI* (London: Hodder and Stoughton, 1977).

5. For the response of industry to incomes policy, see *ibid* and C. J. Crouch, *Class Conflict and the Industrial Relations Crisis* (London: Heinemann, 1977).

6. The CBI's problems in this regard are well set out in M. Moran's *The Politics of Industrial Relations* (London: Macmillan, 1977).

7. B. Weekes, M. Mellish, L. Dickens and J. Lloyd, *Industrial Relations and the Limits of Law* (Oxford: Blackwell, 1975) is the main record of the operation of the Act in practice; see also Moran, *op. cit.*

8. The point is well made in J. Elliott, *Conflict or Co-operation? The Growth of Industrial Democracy* (Lon-

don: Kogan Page, 1978).

9. J. Gennard, *Multi-National Corporations and British Labour* (London: British-North American Committee, 1972).

10. In his *Fort Grunwick* (London: Temple Smith, 1977).

11. For an account of the general role of the City in the British economy, on which this draws, see F. Longstreth, 'The City, Industry and the State', in C. J. Crouch (ed.), *op. cit.*; see also S. Strange, *Sterling and British Policy* (London: Oxford University Press, 1971).

Chapter 7: Labour

1. This question is discussed in detail in J. A. Banks, *Marxist Sociology in Action* (London: Faber, 1970).

2. For a discussion of this and other aspects of class structure in modern Britain, see J. Westergaard and H. Resler, *Class in a Capitalist Society* (London: Heinemann, 1975); and K. Roberts *et al.*, *The Fragmentary Class Structure* (London: Heinemann, 1977).

3. For a more extensive discussion, see C. J. Crouch, 'The Drive for Equality? The Experience of Incomes Policy in Britain', in L. N. Lindberg *et al.* (eds.) *Stress and Contradiction in Modern Capitalism* (Lexington: D. C. Heath, 1975).

4. For full details, see G. S. Bain and R. Price, 'Union Growth Revisited: 1948-1974 in Perspective', *British Journal of Industrial Relations*, XIV, 3, 1976; and G. S. Bain, *The Growth of White-Collar Unionism* (Oxford: Clarendon Press, 1970).

5. *The History of Trade Unionism* (London: Longmans, 1920); see also J. Hughes, *Trade Union Structure and Government* (part one), Research Paper No. 5, Royal Commission on Trade Unions and Employers Associations (London: HMSO, 1966).

6. See R. M. Blackburn, *Union Character and Social*

Class (London: Batsford, 1967); for a highly critical account of this line of reasoning, see G. S. Bain, D. Coates and V. Ellis, *Social Stratification and Trade Unionism* (London: Heinemann, 1973).

7. J. Lovell and B. C. Roberts, *A Short History of the TUC* (London: Macmillan, 1968).

8. See, for example, F. Bealey and S. Parkinson, *Unions in Prosperity*, Hobart Paper No. 6 (London: Institute of Economic Affairs, 1960).

9. I. Richter, in *Political Purpose in Trade Unions* (London: Allen and Unwin, 1973) argues on the basis of a study of the TGWU and the AUEW (formerly the Amalgamated Engineering Union) that unions never really depart from their concentration on collective bargaining, and that their political work is taken much less seriously, being designed largely to ensure that government keeps off their back. This may well be true where the *aspirations* of many trade unionists are concerned. However, over recent years this option has increasingly ceased to be available to unions as they have been forced into politics. This, in turn, gives added scope to those within their ranks who would actually like a political role.

10. See L. Panitch, *Social Democracy and Industrial Militancy* (Cambridge: at the University Press, 1976) for a detailed account of this process.

11. *The Politics of Industrial Relations* (London: Macmillan, 1977).

12. Such a view is expressed by Richter, *op. cit.*

13. I have discussed this issue in more detail in 'Revendications et pouvoir politiques des syndicats pendant les années '70s', *Sociologie du Travail*, 1979.

Chapter 8: Policy Alternatives and Likely Developments

1. Further discussion of this theme will be found in C. J. Crouch, *Class Conflict and the Industrial Relations Crisis* (London: Heinemann, 1977), pp. 262ff.
2. There is a considerable sociological literature on the importance of expectations. For a good account relating it to themes similar to those discussed here, see J. H. Goldthorpe, 'The Current Inflation: towards a Sociological Account', in F. Hirsch and *idem* (eds.), *The Political Economy of Inflation* (London: Martin Robertson, 1978).
3. The most elaborated version of such a policy is S. Holland, *The Socialist Challenge* (London: Quartet, 1975). He does not face squarely the likely implications for collective bargaining, but he does include a high level of worker participation in industrial decision-making within his proposals, which, it might be argued, would in the long run amount to something similar to income restraint.
4. For an extended discussion of this theme see B. Barry, 'The Inflation of Political Economy: a Study of the Political Theory of Some Economists', in L. N. Lindberg and C. S. Maier (eds.), *The Politics and Sociology of Global Inflation and Recession* (Washington DC: Brookings Institution, forthcoming).
5. See the speeches of Sir Keith Joseph, especially *Monetarism is not Enough* (London: Conservative Centre for Policy Studies, 1978).
6. For example, S. Brittan, 'Inflation and Democracy', in F. Hirsch and J. H. Goldthorpe (eds.), *op. cit.*
7. See, on Britain and Japan in particular, R. P. Dore, *British Factory – Japanese Factory* (London: Allen and Unwin, 1973); and, more generally, C. J. Crouch, 'Government-Union Relations as an Aspect of Counter-Inflation Policy', in L. N. Lindberg and C. S. Maier (eds.), *op. cit.*; and *idem*, 'The Changing Role of the

State in Industrial Relations in Western Europe', in *idem* and A. Pizzorno (eds.), *The Resurgence of Class Conflict in Western Europe since 1968*, Volume 2: *Comparative Analyses* (London: Macmillan, 1978).

8. See, on Britain and France in particular, D. Gallie, *In Search of the New Working Class* (Cambridge: at the University Press, 1978); and, more generally, C. J. Crouch, as in note 7.

9. For a more extended discussion see C. J. Crouch in Lindberg and Maier (eds.), *op cit.*

10. J. Bergmann, O. Jacobi and W. Müller-Jentsch, *Gewerkschaften in der Bundesrepublik*, Volume I: *Gewerkschaftliche Lohnpolitik zwischen Mitglieder-interessen und Okonomischen Systemzwangen* (Frankfurt am Main: Aspekte Verlag, 1976).

11. C. J. Crouch, *The Resurgence of Class Conflict . . .*, *op. cit.*, p. 263.

12. M. Moran, *The Politics of Industrial Relations* (London: Macmillan, 1977).

13. For a discussion of this aspect of traditional Toryism and its relation to corporatism, see S. H. Beer, *Modern British Politics* (London: Faber, 1965).

14. The theme of the pre-conditions for trust in work relations is discussed at length in A. Fox, *Beyond Contract: Work, Power and Trust Relations* (London: Faber, 1974). For an analysis of some of the implications of a powerful, decentralized labour movement, see the same author's *Socialism and Shop-Floor Power* (London: Fabian Society, 1978).

Appendix
Some Relevant Statistics

Industrial disputes in the United Kingdom
  since 1945

Year	Number of stoppages		Number of workers involved (in thousands)	Number of days lost (in thousands)
	Total	Percentage reported as official*		
1945	2,293		531	2,835
1946	2,205		526	2,158
1947	1,721		620	2,433
1948	1,759		424	1,944
1949	1,426		433	1,807
1950	1,339		302	1,389
1951	1,719		379	1,694
1952	1,714		415	1,792
1953	1,746		1,370	2,184
1954	1,989		448	2,457
1955	2,419		659	3,781
1956	2,648		507	2,083
1957	2,859		1,356	8,412
1958	2,629		523	3,462
1959	2,093		645	5,270
1960	2,832		814	3,024
1961	2,686	2·2	771	3,046
1962	2,449	3·2	4,420	5,798
1963	2,068	2·4	590	1,755
1964	2,524	2·8	872	2,277
1965	2,354	4·1	868	2,925
1966	1,937	3·1	530	2,398
1967	2,116	5·1	731	2,787
1968	2,378	3·8	2,255	4,690
1969	3,116	3·1	1,654	6,846
1970	3,906	4·1	1,793	10,980
1971	2,228	7·2	1,171	13,551

| Year | Number of stoppages | | Number of workers involved (in thousands) | Number of days lost (in thousands) |
	Total	Percentage reported as official*		
1972	2,497	6·4	1,722	23,909
1973	2,873	4·6	1,513	7,197
1974	2,922	4·3	1,622	14,750
1975	2,282	6·1	789	6,012
1976	2,016	3·4	666	3,284
1977	2,703	2·9	1,155	10,142

* records not kept until 1961

Source: British Labour Statistics: Historical Abstract 1886–1968, Department of Employment, 1971; and *Department of Employment Gazette*, monthly.

Average monthly unemployment rates in the
United Kingdom since 1948 (males and females)

Year	Percentage registered unemployed	Year	Percentage registered unemployed
1948	1·5	1963	2·3
1949	1·5	1964	1·6
1950	1·5	1965	1·4
1951	1·2	1966	1·4
1952	2·0	1967	2·2
1953	1·6	1968	2·4
1954	1·3	1969	2·4
1955	1·0	1970	2·5
1956	1·1	1971	3·4
1957	1·3	1972	3·8
1958	1·9	1973	2·6
1959	2·0	1974*	2·6
1960	1·5	1975	4·3
1961	1·4	1976*	5·6
1962	1·9	1977	6·1

Notes: Figures before 1948 were calculated on a different basis.

Figures are based on persons *registering* as unemployed. Until very recent years this was definitely an under-estimate of total unemployment as many women who became unemployed did not register.

Figures exclude Northern Ireland, where unemployment rates are always higher than in the rest of the UK.

* Figure based on average for eleven months.

Source: British Labour Statistics: Historical Abstract 1886-1968, Department of Employment, 1971; and *Department of Employment Gazette*, monthly.

Indices of retail prices in the United Kingdom
since 1947 (all items; monthly averages)

Index base	Year	Index	Index base	Year	Index
June 17	1948	107·7	January 16	1962	101·6
1947=100	1949	110·7	1962=100	1963	103·6
	1950	114·1		1964	107·0
	1951	124·5		1965	112·1
	1952	135·9		1966	116·5
	1953	140·1		1967	119·4
	1954	142·7		1968	125·0
	1955	149·1		1969	131·8
	Jan. 17			1970	140·2
	1956	153·4		1971	153·4
				1972	164·3
January 17	1956	102·0		1973	179·4
1956=100	1957	105·8		Jan. 15	
	1958	109·0		1974	191·8
	1959	109·6			
	1960	110·7		1974	108·2
	1961	114·5	January 15	1975	134·8
	Jan. 16		1974=100	1976	157·1
	1962	117·5		1977	182·0

Source: British Labour Statistics: Historical Abstract 1886–1968,
Department of Employment, 1971; and *Department of Employment Gazette*, monthly.

Trade-union membership in the United Kingdom
  since 1945

Year	Total labour force (in thousands)[1]	Percentage annual change in labour force	Total trade-union member-ship (in thousands)	Percentage annual change in union membership	Union density[2] (as percentage)
1945	20,400	–	7,875	–	38·6
1948	20,732	–	9,362	–	45·2
1949	20,782	+0·2	9,318	−0·5	44·8
1950	21,055	+1·3	9,289	−0·3	44·1
1951	21,177	+0·6	9,535	+2·6	45·0
1952	21,252	+0·4	9,588	+0·6	45·1
1953	21,352	+0·5	9,527	−0·6	44·6
1954	21,658	+1·4	9,566	+0·4	44·2
1955	21,913	+1·2	9,741	+1·8	44·5
1956	22,180	+1·2	9,778	+0·4	44·1
1957	22,334	+0·7	9,829	+0·5	44·0
1958	22,290	−0·2	9,639	−1·9	43·2
1959	22,429	+0·6	9,623	−0·2	42·9
1960	22,817	+1·7	9,835	+2·2	43·1
1961	23,112	+1·3	9,916	+0·8	42·9
1962	23,432	+1·4	10,014	+1·0	42·7
1963	23,558	+0·5	10,067	+0·5	42·7
1964	23,706	+0·6	10,218	+1·5	43·1
1965	23,920	+0·9	10,325	+1·0	43·2
1966	24,065	+0·6	10,262	−0·6	42·6
1967	23,807	−1·1	10,190	−0·7	42·8
1968	23,667	−0·6	10,193	+0·0	43·1
1969	23,603	−0·3	10,472	+2·7	44·4
1970	23,446	−0·7	11,179	+6·8	47·7
1971	23,231	−0·9	11,127	−0·5	47·9
1972	23,303 (22,959)[3]	+0·3	11,349	+2·0	48·7 (49·4)[3]
1973	23,592 (23,244)[3]	+1·2	11,444	+0·8	48·5 (49·2)[3]
1974	23,689	+0·4	11,755	+2·7	49·6

Year	Total labour force (in thousands)[1]	Percentage annual change in labour force	Total trade-union membership (in thousands)	Percentage annual change in union membership	Union density[2] (as percentage)
	(23,339)[3]				(50·4)[3]
1975	—		12,184	+3·6	(51·73)[3]
	(23,553)[3]	(+0·9)[3]	(12,017)[4]		(51·06)[5]
1976	—		—		
	(23,713)[3]	(+0·7)[3]	(12,376)[4]	(+3·0)[4]	(52·19)[5]

Notes

1. Figures for labour force comprise those in employment and those registered as unemployed.
2. Union density refers to the percentage of labour force in union membership.
3. In 1972 the Department of Employment changed the basis of calculation of the number of people in employment. Figures in brackets are those based on the new form of calculation.
4. In 1975 the Department of Employment changed the basis of calculation of union membership. Figures in brackets are those based on the new form of classification.
5. Figures based on the new forms of classification of *both* labour force and union membership.

Sources: G. S. Bain and R. Price, 'Union Growth Revisited: 1948–1974 in Perspective', *British Journal of Industrial Relations*, November 1976, XIV, 3, 340; updated by the present author for the years after 1974 with data from *Department of Employment Gazette*.

United Kingdom trade-union membership by type and sex of worker, 1948-74

Year and sex	White-collar in thousands	White-collar as percentage	Manual in thousands	Manual as percentage	Total in thousands	Total as percentage
1948						
Male	1,267	33·8	6,410	59·5	7,677	52·9
Female	697	25·4	988	26·0	1,685	25·7
Total	1,964	30·2	7,398	50·7	9,362	45·0
1964						
Male	1,681	33·4	6,329	60·0	8,010	51·4
Female	1,003	24·9	1,206	32·6	2,209	28·6
Total	2,684	29·6	7,534	52·9	10,218	43·1
1970						
Male	2,143	40·0	6,123	63·3	8,266	55·0
Female	1,447	30·7	1,364	35·2	2,811	32·7
Total	3,592	35·2	7,587	56·0	11,179	47·7
1974						
Male	2,593	44·5	5,972	64·7	8,565	56·9
Female	1,629	32·6	1,561	42·1	3,190	36·7
Total	4,263	39·4	7,491	57·9	11,755	49·6

Source: G. S. Bain and R. Price, 'Union Growth Revisited: 1948–1974 in Perspective', *British Journal of Industrial Relations*, November 1976, XIV, 3.

Index